Are you interested in

a course management system that would

save you time & effort?

If the answer is *yes*, **CourseCompass**

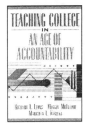    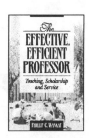 

THE IRIS CENTER
FOR FACULTY ENHANCEMENT
Peabody College at Vanderbilt University

Enhance your course with these free online resources from IRIS!

WHAT'S IRIS?

The IRIS Center for Faculty Enhancement is based at Vanderbilt University's Peabody College and supported through a federal grant. The goal of the IRIS Center is to create course enhancement materials for college faculty who teach pre-service general education teachers, school administrators, school counselors and school nurses.

WHAT RESOURCES DOES IRIS HAVE?

IRIS course enhancement materials are designed to better prepare school personnel to provide an appropriate education to students with disabilities. To achieve this goal, IRIS has created free course enhancement materials for college faculty in the following areas:

● **Accommodations** ● **Behavior** ● **Collaboration** ● **Disability** ● **Diversity** ● **Instruction**

These resources include online interactive modules, case study units, information briefs, student activities, an online dictionary, and a searchable directory of disability-related web sites. These resource materials are designed for use either as supplements to college classes (e.g., homework assignments) or as in-class activities.

STAR LEGACY MODULES

Challenge-based interactive lessons are provided using *STAR Legacy* modules. The following is a list of some of the many modules available on the IRIS website:

- A Clear View: Setting Up Your Classroom for Students with Visual Disabilities
- Who's in Charge? Developing a Comprehensive Behavior Management System
- You're in Charge! Developing A Comprehensive Behavior Management Plan
- Addressing the Revolving Door: How to Retain Your Special Education Teachers
- What Do You See? Perceptions of Disability
- Teachers at the Loom: Culturally and Linguistically Diverse Exceptional Students
- See Jane Read: Teaching Reading to Young Children of Varying Disabilities

CASE STUDIES

IRIS case studies include three levels of cases for a given topic, with each level requiring higher-level analysis and understanding from students.

- Fostering Student Accountability For Classroom Work
- Effective Room Arrangement
- Early Reading
- Norms and Expectations
- Encouraging Appropriate Behavior
- Reading: Word Identification/Fluency, Grades 3-5
- Reading: Comprehension/Vocabulary, Grades 3-5

WEB RESOURCE DIRECTORY

These online directories help faculty members and college students to search by category to find information about websites on the special education or disability topic of their interest.

All IRIS materials are available to faculty at no cost through the IRIS website http://iris.peabody.vanderbilt.edu or on CD by request to the IRIS Center (1-866-626-IRIS).

Instructor's Resource Manual

for

Classroom Assessment
What Teachers Need to Know

Fourth Edition

W. James Popham
University of California, Los Angeles

Boston   New York   San Francisco
Mexico City   Montreal   Toronto   London   Madrid   Munich   Paris
Hong Kong   Singapore   Tokyo   Cape Town   Sydney

ISBN 0-205-43101-1

Printed in the United States of America

10 9 8 7 6 5 4 3 2 1   09 08 07 06 05 04

Table of Contents

INTRODUCTION

This is an *Instructor's Resource Manual (IRM)* for the fourth edition of *Classroom Assessment: What Teachers Need to Know.* I'll frequently use the space-saving abbreviation to refer to the *IRM*. What I want to do in this introduction is briefly describe what you'll find in this manual. Clearly, an *IRM* such as this should make an instructor's tasks more simple. So, if you know what's included in the following pages, you'll surely be able to employ the manual more easily.

Publishers assume, and I suspect they're correct, that busy instructors will typically be more inclined to adopt a textbook if the textbook is accompanied by resources to simplify the teaching and testing responsibilities of the instructor. That is the mission of this *IRM*. I hope it will be successful.

I've used these sorts of *IRMs* myself on numerous occasions, but those manuals were invariably prepared by someone other than the author of the text itself. I always had the feeling that I was looking at support materials prepared by a graduate student in search of extra income. Some of these manuals were quite good. After all, what are graduate students but instructors-in-waiting? Yet, when it was proposed that an *IRM* be prepared for the *third* edition of *Classroom Assessment*, I decided that I wanted to give it a shot myself. A year or two earlier, I had written my first *IRM*, for another measurement textbook. That endeavor made me a "seasoned" preparer of *IRMs*. Now, having been asked to update this IRM for the new, fourth edition of *Classroom Assessment*, I ought to be an old pro at any IRM party. You can judge, after you've used this *IRM*, whether I should have turned the task over to a graduate student.

Since the third edition of *Classroom Assessment* was published, an enormously important federal law was enacted—a law laden with implications for the way that classroom teachers assess their students. Signed by President George W. Bush on January 8, 2002, the *No Child Left Behind Act* (NCLB) might not have registered on any earthquake-detecting Richter Scale, but it seems certain to shake up U.S. publication dramatically. I'm guessing that a 7.0-8.0 Richter reading would be about right.

And because of NCLB's impact on classroom assessment, the fourth edition of *Classroom Assessment* is designed to tackle this issue head-on. Here's the thematic issue I've tried to address in the new edition: *How can classroom assessment most effectively benefit students when carried out in a context dominated by accountability tests?*

For me to have revised a classroom assessment text without taking into consideration NCLB's likely impact on teachers' day-to-day teaching and testing activities would be like getting ready to do a bit of board-surfing without inquiring about the height of the incoming waves. (I have personally surfed on 2-foot waves—with my total stand-up time approximately 10 seconds. I have watched—from a safe distance—skilled surfers ride 20-foot waves. There is a striking difference between 2-footers and 20-footers!)

So your students will find that a fair amount of attention has been given to the implications of NCLB in the fourth edition. I also warned readers, as I am now warning you, that the federal regulations for implementing this significant law may well be modified in the future. Indeed, if the predicted proportions of U.S. public schools actually turn out to be seen as ineffective, I'm predicting that Congress may make some alterations in the law itself, not only in the law's regulations. So, please try to keep abreast of what's happening in NCLB-land. As an instructor, you'll be apt to learn about any major NCLB modifications far earlier than your students. If there are any meaningful changes in what this federal law requires, your students should be let in on those changes.

Innards of an *IRM*

Here's what you'll find in subsequent pages. For each of *Classroom Assessment's* 15 chapters, you'll find the following components:

• Instructor to Instructor: A brief Instructor-to-Instructor section in which I try to relay instructional insights gleaned from my own experiences in teaching classroom assessment courses at UCLA or in school districts. For certain chapters, these instructor-to-instructor introductions are really experience-based musings that may be useful to you. For other chapters, I've simply provided an introduction to the chapter's content other than what's contained in *Classroom Assessment* itself. I've also supplied a brief preview of the suggested activities for the chapter as well as that chapter's test. Finally, there's an answer key provided for the chapter test.

• Chapter Activities: In each chapter there are two or three activities described that you might wish to use with your own students. Each of the activities is based on content treated in that chapter. I've used a good many of these activities over the years. I am definitely *not* recommending that you use all of the suggested activities in a chapter. Indeed, you might choose to use none. However, *if* you wish to have your students engage in either some small-group or some individual exercises, these activities may give you a few ideas. The activities, of course, are eminently modifiable. Each suggested activity is identified by the following symbols: ◆ ◆ ◆ .

• Chapter Tests: For each chapter there is also a test. You'll find those tests consist of different sorts of test items. I am *not* recommending that you use all of these tests. In many instances, a chapter test might not even be sensible. However, *if* you want to employ a chapter test, there's one available.

The chapter tests are all presented on un-numbered pages, thereby rendering them more readily photocopiable. There are no spaces provided for students' names on the chapter tests, in case you might wish to have students write their names on the backs of any test. There are also no designations in any test's directions regarding how many items there are in the test. This will allow you to shorten any test simply by deleting its final items so that, for example, a ten-item test is transformed into a five-item test, and so on. If you reduce a ten-item test to a *one*-item test, you've probably pruned a bit too ruthlessly!

• Mid-Course Examination: There is also a mid-course exam and a final exam provided near the end of the *IRM*. Let me explain about the nature of those two tests. I think it will help you understand why I chose to design them as I did and, perhaps more importantly, how I view a course on classroom assessment for experienced teachers or prospective teachers.

A few paragraphs earlier, I proclaimed with thinly masked pride, that I was a seasoned developer of *IRMs*. The text for which I'd done my ground-breaking *IRM* work was a book about assessment that would typically be used in doctoral or master's degree programs for individuals preparing to become educational administrators, curriculum specialists, and so on. For that textbook's *IRM*, I had created a 50-item mid-course and a 100-item final exam using multiple binary-choice items. When I was getting ready to write this new *IRM*, that is, the *IRM* for *Classroom*

Assessment, I fully intended to create the same kinds of tests that I had generated for the earlier IRM. After all, I knew how!

But the closer I got to doing it, the less comfortable I became with the prospect. You see, to create a 100-item exam on a 15-chapter book, one is often obliged to focus on fairly fine-grained bits of truth. And some of those fine-grained bits of truth, although you can create suitable items dealing with them, deal with content more subtle than is suggested by *Classroom Assessment's* subtitle, namely, *What Teachers Need to Know*!

Thus, I focused more on the major concepts I want classroom teachers to comprehend. And in doing so, I found myself moving toward shorter and different sorts of exams. I ended up creating a pair of exams consisting exclusively of multiple-choice items. There is a 25-item mid-course examination on pages 99-103. It is based on Chapter 1 through Chapter 7. On pages 105-115 you will find a 50-item final examination. It covers content in all 15 chapters.

Frankly, I do not think either of these exams is all that difficult. I suspect that you will agree. But I was not trying to create tests that would lead to fine-grained norm-referenced interpretations. I just wanted exams that would indicate whether a student taking a classroom assessment course had learned the most important points about educational testing that classroom teachers *really need to know*.

In that regard, throughout *Classroom Assessment* the reader will frequently find sets of concepts, rules, or activities to be understood such as three kinds of validity evidence, five general item-writing commandments, and eight steps to be taken in creating a Likert self-report inventory. Now, given that I was only intending to devote approximately three multiple-choice items (in the mid-course and final exams) to each chapter, you'll find I often created items asking the student to identify an answer option that was *not* a member of the set of "things" treated in a chapter. This approach, although it typically forces the student to look for negative instances, is a much more efficient way to see if the student recognizes at least the bulk of chapter-identified content. If you use either or both of the *IRM's* exams in your own classes, you may wish to call your students' attention to the frequent presence of item-stems in which a non-instance is sought.

Incidentally, if you wish to toughen up either examination, I suggest that you simply add one or more essay items to either the mid-course or final examinations. Those essay items, of course, should deal with the content that you stressed as you taught the course.

• <u>Answer Keys for Mid-Course and Final Examinations</u>: On page 117, answer keys for both the mid-course and final examinations are presented.

• <u>Classroom Assessment Confidence Inventory</u>: A classroom assessment confidence inventory consisting of 20 items is presented on pages 119-120. This affective inventory can be used on a pre-instruction and post-instruction basis to see if, as a group, your students' confidence in carrying out assessment-related activities has been augmented. The inventory should, of course, be administered anonymously as pointed out in Chapter 10 of *Classroom Assessment*.

Using *Classroom Assessment's* Chapter Features

Several features of *Classroom Assessment's* chapters might be employed instructionally if you wish to do so. For example, in each chapter any word or phrase that is defined in the *end-of-book glossary* is glossed and bold-faced when it first appears in the text. You could certainly devise some sort of continuing activity with your students calling for them to master the chapter's glossary entries, then be prepared to display that mastery in class during various sorts of total-group, small-group, or paired-partner activities.

Whereas each *chapter summary* attempts to capture the important elements treated in the chapter, that summary is immediately preceded by a *"What Do Classroom Teachers Really Need to Know About (the chapter's focus)?"* You might find that either or both of these sections could routinely help solidify your students' understanding of a chapter's emphases. The chapter's *self-check* exercises, of course, ought to help your students master at least one or two of the chapter's important concepts. In each chapter there's a description of a fictitious teacher in a classroom situation related to one or more of the topics addressed in that chapter. These inserts are given a *Decision Time* label because that's what a reader is asked to do: make a decision. Readers are urged to consider what kind of decision they would make if they found themselves in a similar situation. You might use some of these *Decision-Time* exercises as stimuli for class discussions.

Every chapter also contains a *Parent Talk* insert and attempts to get teachers to consider how best to communicate with important players in the educational game, namely, students' parents. In recent years I've become sufficiently convinced that we need to promote parents' assessment literacy that I've actually written a book about educational testing just for parents. If you share my belief about parents' importance in the assessment arena, I hope you'll find a way to use the *Parent Talk* inserts in the book's chapters.

A new feature in the current edition of *Classroom Assessment* is a chapter insert entitled: But what does this have to do with *teaching*? These inserts represent a tangible effort to keep teachers aware of the strong links between testing and teaching. I hope you'll find opportunities to support the idea that the chief payoff of first-rate classroom assessment is a meaningful improvement in the level of student learning.

Each chapter also contains *Ponder Time* questions that you may want to use as catalysts for post-chapter discussions. In teaching this sort of course for prospective and seasoned teachers, I try very hard to get my students talking (and thinking) about each chapter's contents.

Finally, three sets of materials are cited at the close of most chapters. First off, there's *Additional Stuff*, that is, books and journal articles containing content relevant to what's treated in the chapter. Then there's *Nonprint Stuff* that, for many chapters, identifies videotapes or audiotapes I thought were germane to the chapter's content. Finally, there's a listing of *Cyber Stuff* web sites that students with a computer, a bit of computer moxie, and a dash of electrical power can visit. I'm not a genuinely competent Internet person, so I assure you the *Cyber Stuff* entries were obtained only after substantial investments on my part of time, errors, and unconstrained cursing. I hope your computer-capable students will while away the hours messing around with those charming little www_s!

Incidentally, I visited (electronically) each of the listed web sites just before sending the fourth edition of *Classroom Assessment* off to the publisher. All of the web sites were working at that point. By the time you use the book with your own students, of course, who knows?

Thanks

  I want to express my appreciation to Dolly Bulquerin, word-processing wizard, who transformed my hand-written ideas for the revision of this *IRM* into respectable, camera-ready copy. As in all of my major writing projects during the past decade, her help has been truly terrific.

Good Luck

  Classroom assessment has, in recent years, become a popular focus for textbook writers and purveyors of staff development programs. That's great. I think that teachers who know the things set forth in this book or the books of my colleagues will, as a consequence, be better teachers. And, of course, their students will, therefore, learn more and learn it better. And that is why most of us went into education in the first place.

  Good luck.

W.J.P.
2004

CHAPTER 1

WHY DO TEACHERS NEED TO KNOW ABOUT ASSESSMENT?

Instructor to Instructor

Firing Up the Troops

If you're teaching a classroom-assessment course, whether your students are prospective teachers or experienced classroom teachers, you'll almost certainly need to do at least some sort of motivational job to get your students to approach the course with suitable zeal.

More often than not, at least in my experience, most students take courses because they are required to do so. Teacher education students typically enroll in a classroom-assessment course either because it is a licensure requirement or because the student's advisor urged that the course be taken. As I was revising this *IRM*, only about a dozen states *required* prospective teachers to complete a measurement course. That's not many.

And experienced teachers might sign up for a classroom assessment course as part of a degree program or, increasingly, because officials of a school district have decided that the district's educators need a dose of classroom assessment. Teachers who are directed to take a course, even though it might be billed as a professional development course, are rarely jubilant about that prospect. Having taught such indifferent, reluctant, or sometimes hostile teachers, I know.

At any rate, I encourage you *not* to assume that your students are breathlessly waiting to lap up all the assessment truths you are prepared to toss their way. And, if you agree, this means you need to try to bolster my efforts in Chapter 1 to get readers to recognize the importance of learning about classroom assessment. Part of the rationale for mastering the content you'll be treating in Chapter 1 is fairly lofty, that is, a competent educational professional these days simply must know something about assessment because students' test scores are the chief indicators of educational quality. But I've found in my own courses that the most effective hook for my students is the recognition that this *assessment* content can make them more effective *teachers*.

Indeed, in the fourth edition of *Classroom Assessment*, you'll find that I often bang away at that bongo, namely, the linkage between testing and teaching. Happily, not only is the potential for classroom assessment's *instructional* payoff a sound motivational ploy—it happens to be the truth. So, I hope you'll spend at least some early-on time trying to get your students energized so they'll tackle the textbook's content with enthusiasm. It really is important content. And teachers who are better classroom assessors will almost certainly be better teachers. Your students need to realize it.

The chapter's Likert self-test about teaching, if you wish to use it for your entire class, ought to be completed at the very outset of the course, for instance, during the first 5-10 minutes of your first class session. You can decide, of course, whether you'll be asking students to fill out the same self-test at the course's conclusion. It's more convenient for students, of course, if you can photocopy the self-test, then pass it out so your students don't need to mark up their "precious" book. (Well, *I* think it is!)

1

NCLB Nervousness

As time goes by, it becomes increasingly unlikely that educators or educators-in-training have not heard of the *No Child Left Behind Act* (NCLB). To most educators, it is a truly terrifying federal law. That's because if students do not annually make really substantial improvements in their test scores, then a school (and, by implication, that school's teachers) will be regarded as a failing school. Flocks of euphemistic labels will be employed to describe schools whose students fail to make "adequate yearly progress," but whatever the designation, poor performing schools will be regarded as poor performing schools. Few teachers yearn to be working in such a school.

Thus, if you can assure your students that they'll be learning about the likely impact of NCLB on their day-in, day-out activities, it seems that you'll have baited your motivational hook properly. Only teachers these days who are genuinely catatonic will be unconcerned about NCLB—particularly in the assessment-linked accountability provisions of that federal law. The fourth edition of *Classroom Assessment* attempts to lay out the most salient features of this often intimidating law.

What's Coming

Many students, especially those inclined to engage in some sort of cognition, like to know what's coming in a course or in a textbook. Toward the end of Chapter 1, I spell out three content foci for the whole book, namely, (1) constructing classroom assessments, (2) using assessment devices constructed by others, and (3) planning instruction based on assessments that can help guide a teacher's instructional decision-making. Whenever I teach a *full-length* course on classroom assessment (Sometimes, for professional development programs, only parts of the content in *Classroom Assessment* are treated.), I always try to keep these three emphases clearly in front of my students. They may still get lost along the way, of course, but I try hard to let them know where they're heading.

Number Fear

Based on my experience, somewhere around 42.74% of the students who take a classroom assessment course are afraid that its numerical orientation will overwhelm them. I can't be too sure about the actual percent, however, because the sampling error on my survey is plus-or-minus 99%. But, data notwithstanding, it's pretty clear that a good many of your students may be intimidated by what they believe will be a course that oozes quantitative complexity.

I've found it helpful to address these numerical phobics early in the course. The truth, of course, is that a solid course in classroom assessment could probably be taught that never asked folks to do much more than compute an arithmetic mean. I certainly believe that the majority of the key concepts associated with classroom assessment can be mastered without ever moving beyond fifth-grade math. Usually, after I extol the virtues of a math-free approach to assessment early in a course, I see a half-dozen or so of my students happily pocket their tranquilizers.

What About Parents?

Toward the end of Chapter 1, I make a modest pitch for readers to think about sharing their newly acquired knowledge about educational assessment with their students' parents. I'm not sure if you agree with my position on this issue. But, for me, the past decade has inclined me to think that educators blunder if they don't familiarize the larger community, and especially their students' parents, with key concepts linked to educational assessment.

An assessment-literate group of parents can be a potent force in supporting a teacher's instructional efforts and, in addition, in combating serious misuses of educational assessment. I've recently been viewing considerable parent-expressed distress about educational testing, especially high-stakes testing, on several of the internet listserves (for example, the Assessment Reform Network Listserve, ARN-L@listsrva CUA EDU). The level of dissatisfaction with educational testing registered by many parents is quite striking. Yet, in many instances these distressed parents have never been given even rudimentary information about the tests against which they rail. I'd like to see that situation change. So, I now always encourage my classroom assessment students to "spread the word" to parents, not only parents of their own students (if they're already teaching), but also to all parents of the students in their school. If you concur with this view, then you'll have ample opportunities throughout the course to encourage your students to think about this possibility.

In Sum

Summing up, I think the chief instructional task in connection with Chapter 1 is to help your students come up with a solid, defensible answer to the question that constitutes the chapter's title, that is, "Why do teachers need to know about assessment?"

Activities

Two of the possible chapter activities suggested for Chapter 1 (Remember, such activities are preceded by this designation: ♦ ♦ ♦.) deal with the reasons why a teacher should learn about classroom assessment. The third possible chapter activity is related to NCLB. At most, I'd use only one activity for this chapter's content. I'd certainly not use both and, if pressed for time, would probably use none.

Chapter Test

Because this is the initial chapter in the book, and because it is dominantly a motivation-focused chapter, I'm not sure I'd use a test at the chapter's close. Oh, I might toss it out as a self-test *along with* the answer key, but that's about it. But I promised a chapter test for each of the book's 15 chapters. And, if I skipped Chapter 1, I could never catch up!

Answer Key. 1: Traditional, 2: Today's, 3: Neither, 4: Traditional, 5: Today's, 6: Traditional, 7: Neither, 8: Traditional, 9: Traditional (But because this reason might be readily confused with Today's reason that assessment data are being increasingly used in the evaluation of teachers, a Today's answer is also correct. I am so soft!), 10: Traditional.

Chapter Activities

◆◆◆ Convincing Colleagues

Split your students into small groups, then ask each group to pretend it must make an oral presentation at a school faculty meeting to encourage teachers to take an eight-week extension course, one class per week, in classroom assessment offered by a nearby university. Each subgroup should decide how to put forward the most convincing case so that as many as possible of the school's teachers will sign up for the course. Allow about 10-15 minutes for the subgroups to plan their presentations.

Then, having assigned numbers to each of the subgroups, and placed each of those numbers on separate slips of paper, have one of your students select a number. The subgroup selected should then make its presentation to the remaining students who are, at that point, to assume the roles of teachers at a faculty meeting. You may wish to allow the "teachers" to ask questions at the close of the subgroup's presentation.

After the subgroup's presentation, you may wish to lead a full-class discussion to consider the strong and weak points of the chosen subgroup's presentation. Because all students will have, in their own subgroup, previously taken part in dealing with the reasons for teachers to take a classroom assessment course, this improvement-focused discussion can sometimes become fairly lively.

◆◆◆ Push a Partner

Require students to pair up, then ask *each* person to silently think through how to persuade a teacher to read a book about classroom assessment such as the enthralling textbook your students are now using. After about five minutes, ask students to explain, in turn, to their partner why that person should learn about classroom assessment. After *both* partners have completed their explanations, encourage them to collaboratively determine which points (in both presentations) would be the most persuasive to a typical teacher.

◆◆◆ NCLB Understandings

Ask your students at the close of one class to find out "what the world knows about NCLB." Each student should interview several people (other than the student's classmates) to discover people's perceptions regarding why NCLB was enacted, how it works, and whether it is a good or bad law.

At the beginning of the next class, your students should describe people's views of NCLB (including, people's unawareness of the law). Views of laypeople and educators could be contrasted to see if any important differences in perceptions exist.

CHAPTER 1 TEST

Directions: In this chapter four *Traditional* reasons and three of *Today's* reasons were given for teachers to learn how to assess students. Please read each of the fictional statements below, then classify it, by making an appropriate response, as a *Traditional Reason*, a *Today's Reason*, or *Neither One*. Certain of the reasons may be used more than once or not at all.

Teachers should learn about classroom assessment:	Traditional Reason	Today's Reason	Neither One
1. "So they can figure out if they're doing a dazzling or a dismal job of teaching."	O	O	O
2. "So they have a better idea about where their instruction should be heading."	O	O	O
3. "So parents will regard teachers as more complete professionals."	O	O	O
4. "So when grading time comes around, a student's grade will be based on solid evidence of achievement."	O	O	O
5. "So that the public's perceptions of a school's effectiveness will be more accurate."	O	O	O
6. "So they can make more accurate, diagnostically based decisions about their students' status."	O	O	O
7. "So they can, when the timing is appropriate, communicate directly with families via the internet."	O	O	O
8. "So they can systematically keep track of their students' progress."	O	O	O
9. "So they can determine their personal instructional effectiveness."	O	O	O
10. "So the initial entry knowledge and skills of students can be accurately ascertained."	O	O	O

CHAPTER 2

RELIABILITY OF ASSESSMENT

Instructor to Instructor

"Patience, People!"

Because Chapter 2 is the first truly *substantive* chapter of the book—not counting the Chapter 1 "warm-'em-up" focus, some of my students get a bit impatient because they are not immediately digging into the viscera of items for their own classroom tests. A few of my students, the most candid ones to be sure, have expressed serious annoyance that they must deal with this "theoretical stuff about reliability."

When I first heard such carping, and it came from some seasoned classroom teachers, I automatically became a mite defensive. I told those carpers that "validity, reliability, and absence-of-bias are the cornerstones of classroom tests." My carpers quieted down, of course. Even experienced teachers know who's running a classroom assessment course. Yet, as I reflected on that early incident, I realized that I could most likely have forestalled such a response had I been more proactive about introducing the content of Chapters 2, 3, and 4. Since that time, I've introduced Chapter 2 differently (at the time I assign it) and, so far, it's worked charm-like.

Here's how I do it. I tell my students that one of the key things they'll learn in the course is how to construct their own classroom tests. And, in fact, starting with Chapter 5 dealing with what to assess and how to assess it, there are seven chapters in a row that explicitly treat the development and refinement of classroom tests. However, to make those seven chapters pay off, a reader of *Classroom Assessment* really needs to be able to judge the quality of classroom tests. And that's what Chapters 3, 4, and 5 do. They'll provide a set of important, and thoroughly *understandable*, factors by which teachers can tell whether their classroom tests are dazzlers or duds.

Accordingly, I try to head off the perception that Chapter 2 and the next two chapters represent "theoretical" measurement content that has little real-world relevance. In short, I ask my class for a three-chapter excursion into *patience*. I point out that people who can deal with long-term gratification are often the most successful folks around. How else would we have put men on the moon? Actually, I don't infuse moon-walking or blatant patriotism into my plea for patience but, if necessary, I would do so in a measurement minute!

Much Ado

Actually, as I close out this chapter with a section about what classroom teachers really need to know about reliability, I suggest that it's not all that much. I surely don't think that teachers need to compute reliability coefficients for their own classroom tests. Yet, and there's a bit of a balancing act required here, I *do* want teachers to understand some of the important ideas related to reliability. For example, the *imprecision of educational measurement* is such a significant concept that teachers should surely carry it away from this chapter. Do anything you can to help your students recognize the imprecise nature of the classroom assessments they'll be creating. A solid look at the standard error of measurement will typically be useful in reinforcing this insight.

In short, although the chapter doesn't urge readers to scurry forth with an anointed assignment to roll up a pile of reliability coefficients for their own tests, the topics treated in Chapter 2 are important ones. It is these topics that they need to master. Try to make them recognize this.

Not too long ago, Nebraska educators were urged to create local district-level assessments to determine if students had mastered the skills and knowledge they were supposed to learn. However, in order to increase the likelihood that those locally developed assessments would be good ones, district educators were asked to send their tests through all sorts of serious technical scrutiny. Many Nebraska educators reported that because of the need to collect exotic reliability indicators (Does every teacher really want to compute a Kuder-Richardson reliability coefficient?), insufficient time was available for instructionally relevant decision-making. Sensibly, Nebraska education officials relaxed the stringency of their requirements for technical displays of assessment reliability.

By the way, in the third edition of *Classroom Assessment*, I had only described the computation of a split-half reliability coefficient (and the nifty Spearman-Brown Prophecy Formula that's used with it) at the chapter's conclusion—as part of a Self-Check Key. Well, two external reviewers of the third edition urged that I move it up, into the chapter itself. Being an obliging author, and because I thought the reviewers were correct, that topic is now treated in the chapter.

Categorization Fun

Much of my students appear to enjoy the rather tidy division of reliability evidence into three categories. Indeed, the self-test for Chapter 2 and the Chapter 2 test that you'll find in a page or two are largely based on this tripartite classification model. I always have fun getting my students to become facile in identifying different types of reliability evidence. I hope you do too. But the IRM's chapter test also asks students to display their understanding of several other important concepts in the chapter. In my mind, the content addressed in the chapter test's five short-answer items is meaningfully more important than the three-category split among types of reliability evidence.

Activities

There are three chapter activities offered for Chapter 2. All three concentrate on having your students arrive at insights regarding the chapter's content by generating explanations or examples of this content. The first activity is based on the three-way split of reliability evidence described in the chapter. The second activity focuses on the imprecision of educational measurement. The final activity asks students to come up with an explanation *for parents* of the meaning of a standard error of measurement. This last activity, of the three, is surely the most challenging!

Chapter Test

This two-part test starts off with five multiple-choice items (three options per item) and closes out with five short-answer items.

Answer Key. 1: Alternate Forms; 2: Stability (This is a tough choice because the board's policy is so bizarre. A case could be made for alternate-forms evidence because of the original and alternate forms.); 3: Internal Consistency; 4: Internal Consistency; 5: Stability; 6: Classification-consistency reliability is, as the label suggests, a representation of the proportion of students who are classified identically on two different test forms or two different administrations of the same test; 7, 8, and 9 are answered correctly if the student's response represents a reasonable paraphrase of the term's definition in the end-of-book glossary; 10: For this item, a correct response should definitely include the idea that the standard error of measurement is focused on the consistency of an individual student's performances rather than a group-focused reliability estimate such as those seen in the three types of reliability evidence described in the chapter.

Chapter Activities

♦♦♦ **Pick an Approach**

Ask your students to organize themselves into two-person or three-person teams. Then each team should generate five brief written vignettes in which one of the three types of reliability evidence would be needed for large-scale assessment (not classroom assessment). After allowing sufficient preparation time, each team should exchange its vignettes (orally or in written form) with another team to see if that second team can determine which form of evidence would be most appropriate for each of the vignettes. The vignettes are apt to resemble those you will find in the IRM's test for this chapter.

♦♦♦ **It Ain't Exact, and Here's Why**

Ask students to spend a few moments thinking through how they would explain to a classroom teacher why it is not wise to place much faith in the precision of educational testing. Then have students trade off explanations, that is, have students explain to each other why unwarranted belief in assessment's precision of measurement is unwise.

♦♦♦ **The Standard Error of Parenting**

Because the standard error of measurement is a useful concept for helping teachers—*and parents*—recognize the imprecision of educational testing, see if your students can come up with an understandable explanation to a parent of what a standard error of measurement actually is.

Again, split the class into subgroups, then allow each group to arrive at a *parent-comprehensible* explanation of what a standard measurement is. After the groups are ready, randomly call on one or two subgroups to provide their explanations for the rest of the class who, at that point, pretend to be parents.

CHAPTER 2 TEST

Part I

> Directions: For the first five items, read the description of the kind of reliability evidence that seems to be needed, then decide which kind of reliability evidence should be sought by circling the letter of the correct answer from the three options given.

1. A commercial testing company has developed a brand new test intended to measure the mathematics skills of students who possess limited English proficiency. Because there are three different forms of the test at each of six grade levels, and teachers are encouraged to use all three forms during the year, the sales representatives of the company are demanding reliability evidence (from technical personnel) that will best help them market the new test. What kind of reliability evidence seems most useful in this situation?

    A. Stability   B.   Alternate-Forms   C.   Internal Consistency

2. A school district's testing office has been directed to construct a basic skills test in language arts that can be taken at any point during an extensive three-month summer session by eighth-grade students who failed an earlier test. By district policy, the earlier test must be passed before students can enroll in the ninth grade. The school board's policy, however, says that the student can choose the occasion (one time per student) when an alternate test is administered. Critics of the policy fear that there will be striking differences in students' performances depending on *when* they choose to be tested with the alternate test. What kind of reliability evidence seems most needed in this setting?

    A. Stability   B.   Alternate-Forms   C.   Internal Consistency

3. A Texas school superintendent in a district near the Mexican border has asked his assessment specialist, Mr. Chavez, to create a brief test that will provide the district's educators with a general idea of immigrant students' ability to read English. Mr. Chavez builds a 20-item test, administered with the use of audiotaped directions in Spanish. All of the items, however, are written in English. The test's overall function is to yield a single estimate of a Spanish-speaking student's ability to read English. What kind of reliability evidence would be most informative in this situation?

    A. Stability   B.   Alternate-Forms   C.   Internal Consistency

4. A test-contracting firm has agreed to create a three-part social studies test intended to measure sixth-graders' knowledge of geography, government, and history. The test is to be used as a statewide assessment to govern the allocation of staff-development funds for elementary teachers. Because of limitations in administration time, only 15 items are allowed for each of the three content areas. If the test-development firm wants to know if its three test sub-sections are measuring with suitable consistency what they are supposed to be measuring, what kind of reliability evidence would be best?

    A. Stability   B.   Alternate-Forms   C.   Internal Consistency

5.   Based on a new state law, high-school students are going to be permitted to take a basic skills graduation test, administered via a computer, at any time during a three-week test-administration window. Only one version of the test will be available each year, but will be substantially revised the following year. What kind of reliability evidence seems most needed here for each year's test?

        A.   Stability   B.   Alternate-Forms   C.   Internal Consistency

Part II

Directions: Answer each of the following five questions in the spaces provided.

6.   What is meant by *classification-consistency reliability*? _____
        _____
        _____
        _____

7.   Briefly, what is *stability reliability*? _____
        _____
        _____
        _____

8.   Briefly, what is *alternate-form reliability*? _____
        _____
        _____
        _____

9.   Briefly, what is *internal-consistency reliability*? _____
        _____
        _____
        _____

10.   In a sentence or two, explain how the standard error of measurement is different than a reliability coefficient. _____
        _____
        _____
        _____

CHAPTER 3

VALIDITY

Instructor to Instructor

Where Liveth Validity?

Many educators, indeed, I'd be willing to say *most* educators, regard validity as a commodity that resides in a test. This is why so many people talk about a "valid test." But, of course, that's wrong. What's valid or invalid is the inference about an examinee based on the examinee's test performance.

When I teach a classroom assessment course, my primary effort regarding validity is to get my students to realize that it is the inference (or interpretation) whose validity is under consideration—and that *people make judgments* about the validity of score-based inferences. If my students really arrive at that understanding (and some never do), then the whole approach to validity based on diverse kinds of evidence, and building a powerful validity argument, begins to make sense. But it's a tough sell. Most people have heard the expression "valid test" for so many years that they really do find it tough to abandon the idea that validity exists, perhaps unseen like people's souls, in the tests themselves. My emphasis when I treat validity is to encourage the kind of thinking about validity that is endorsed in the 1999 *Standards* and in earlier versions of that important set of guidelines.

Blessed Be Trinities

Three-way splits are so delightful from an instructional and an assessment perspective. With three categories, ideally discrete and mutually exclusive ones, there are so many delightful categorization exercises in which an instructor can engage.

Well, I'm just as susceptible to the lure of tripartite divisions as the next instructor. Accordingly, I enjoy seeing if students can become skilled in distinguishing among the three kinds of validity evidence described in the chapter (content-related, criterion-related, and construct-related). Half of the end-of-chapter self-check consists of items based on the differences among these three varieties of validity evidence. You'll also discover that the Chapter 3 test you'll find a few pages later in this IRM closes out with five multiple-choice items about the different kinds of validity evidence.

But please remember that your students need to recognize the different kinds of validity evidence are simply contributors to a *validity argument* that will permit someone to *judge* whether a specific score-based interpretation about a student (or students) is valid.

The Consequential Conundrum

The consequences of educational tests are clearly important. Superb tests that, when used, cause harm to students should clearly not be used in such a way. But the consequences of a test's usage, in my view, should not be imposed on what is, otherwise, a fairly clear notion that validity refers to the judged accuracy of score-based inferences. That's why I think the concept of "consequential validity" is not helpful.

11

Some first-rate measurement folks, however, believe that "consequential validity" is a powerful idea. I don't know how you personally come down on this issue. The summer 1997 issue of *Educational Measurement: Issues and Practice* features four conflicting essays on this topic. If you haven't already arrived at an intractable position regarding the virtues of consequential validity, you might find those essays helpful.

I think classroom teachers ought to know that the consequences of using a given test are often terribly important. I'd prefer to stop there, rather than confusing them with another take on what validity really means. Clearly, it's your choice.

Activities

There are two activities suggested as possibilities for this chapter. The first deals with the most important kind of validity evidence about which classroom teachers should be concerned, namely, content-related evidence of validity. It is a fairly time-consuming activity, having taken my students about an hour whenever I've used such an activity.

The second activity focuses on an effort to have students verbalize, and hopefully understand, why any classroom teacher ought to care about the concept of validity. If enough good arguments are voiced, there may be some honest-to-goodness convincing taking place with your very own students.

Chapter Test

The test for this chapter is a 10-item affair that starts off with five short-answer items dealing with, in order, the following five concepts: (1) the difference between predictive and concurrent forms of criterion-related validity evidence; (2) "consequential validity's" potential shortcomings; (3) the relationship between reliability and validity; (4) "face validity;" and (5) one form of construct-related validity evidence based on a classroom intervention. The final five items in the chapter's test, all multiple-choice in nature, call for students to distinguish among the three kinds of validity evidence described in the chapter.

Answer Key. 1: The key difference is the duration of time between the administration of the predictor test and the collection of the criterion variable. Concurrent criterion-related evidence of validity, as suggested by its title, is gathered almost immediately. Predictive criterion-related evidence is gathered after a much longer interval., 2: Because the uses or misuses of a test's results, that is, the *consequences* of its usage, are not directly relevant to the accuracy of a score-based inference about a student's status with respect to the assessment domain represented by a test., 3: Rarely can a teacher make valid interpretations from an unreliable test. For instance, if a set of stability evidence indicates that students' scores are bouncing all over when the test is administered on different occasions, it is unlikely that an accurate score-based inference can be based on any given performance by students., 4: Because a test *appears* to measure the assessment domain it is supposed to represent, this does not necessarily mean that the test actually does. For instance, a test might look like a mathematics test, but turn out to be based more on students' abilities to *read* the test's word problems than students' ability to display the mathematics skills called for in those word problems., 5: The easiest way for a classroom teacher to carry out an intervention validity study is to (1) pretest student, (2) instruct students to master the knowledge and/or skill being tested, then (3) posttest students. Instructed students should significantly outperform uninstructed students, so it could be predicted that posttest scores will be meaningfully superior to pretest scores., 6: Construct-related evidence of validity (based on a related-measures approach), 7: Content-related evidence of validity, 8: Criterion-related evidence of validity (of the predictive variety), 9: None of the above (Martin was computing reliability coefficients of the stability sort.), 10: Content-related evidence of validity.

Chapter Activities

♦♦♦ Is Alignment a Four-Letter Word?

This activity focuses on the kind of content-related evidence of validity that, of the three types of validity evidence, is the most apt to be collected by classroom teachers. The activity requires small-group generation of items that may/may not be used to help determine if a student has mastered a particular content standard.

I have supplied two content standards here, both based on an actual set of content standards for middle schools. If you prefer to generate your own content standards for this activity, please do so. You have a better sense of what kinds of content standards will be suitable for your own students.

I chose two content standards, one in mathematics and one in language arts, because it is likely that most students in a classroom assessment course will be familiar with the content of those two subject matters. I selected a more general, less constrictive language arts content standard and a more restrictive mathematics content standard. The difference in the two content standards' specificity will, in general, lead your students toward an important insight regarding the difficulty of reviewing the rigor with which a test item meshes with a loosely defined content standard.

Content Standards for Seventh Graders

Language Arts: students will become knowledgeable regarding the most common conventions associated with written English, for example, spelling, capitalization, punctuation, and word usage.

Mathematics: the student will be able to carry out successfully the four basic computation operations (namely, addition, subtraction, multiplication, and division). The difficulty of these tasks should coincide with that called for in routine, age-appropriate arithmetic tasks.

After distributing these two content standards (or those you provide) to your students, split the students into subgroups and ask each subgroup to construct at least four items that, at least from a cursory inspection, could be regarded as being "aligned" with each of the two content standards. That is, each subgroup should create at least eight items in all. Thereafter, as you direct, each group should exchange its two sets of items with another group. At that point, each item should be reviewed by the other group using the following content-focused review question:

Item-Review Question: Will students' responses to this item, in concert with their responses to other items, contribute to a valid inference regarding whether a student has mastered the content standard to which the item is linked? (Yes, No, or Uncertain)

After all items have been subjected to this kind of content-focused item review, you might wish to focus on items about which there were substantial disagreements regarding their alignment with the content standard. You might also want to determine if the more restrictive nature of the mathematics content standard resulted in alignment differences unlike those seen for the less restrictive language arts content standard. Indeed, an open discussion of the item-writing and item-reviewing activities is likely to lead to other issues worth your students' consideration.

♦♦♦ Why Care About Validity?

Split your students into pairs, then for five minutes allow each student to prepare as persuasive an argument as possible to convince a classroom teacher that teachers need to understand the concept of assessment validity. After five minutes of preparation time, each pair should flip a coin to see who goes first, then *both* pair-members should, in turn, provide their explanation to their counterpart. During those explanations, the person receiving the persuasive argument should assume the role of a *beginning* classroom teacher.

After the persuasive efforts have been concluded, you might wish to have some students identify arguments that they thought were especially convincing as well as those they regarded as somewhat ineffectual.

CHAPTER 3 TEST

1. What is the chief difference between *predictive* criterion-related validity evidence and *concurrent* criterion-related validity evidence?

    _____

    _____

    _____

2. Why was it suggested in the chapter that "consequential validity," although a well-intentioned concept, should not be regarded as a legitimate form of validity evidence?

    _____

    _____

    _____

3. If a classroom test yields results that are quite unreliable, how likely is it that a teacher will be able to arrive at valid score-based inferences about a student's status? Why?

    _____

    _____

    _____

4. How could a classroom test that is "face valid" lead a teacher to make inaccurate inferences about students?

    _____

    _____

    _____

5. The chapter described three types of studies that could be used to support a validity argument focused on construct-related evidence. Briefly, how could a simple *intervention study* be implemented by a classroom teacher to support the validity of inferences based on a particular test?

    _____

    _____

    _____

6. A middle-grade social studies teacher, Mr. Graves, has created a 40-item test covering what she believes is supposed to be taught by middle-grade social studies teachers. As students conclude their middle-school educations, they must complete (according to district policy) a basic skills test in reading, mathematics, and language arts. Because the scores for all of the school's students are available to her, Ms. Graves computes correlation coefficients for her students' scores on her own social studies test versus each of the three district-required tests. She finds only moderate correlations between her 40-item social studies test and the other three tests. Thus, she argues that her test is, sensibly, measuring something other than reading, mathematics, and language arts.

    A. Content-related evidence of validity   C. Construct-related evidence of validity
    B. Criterion-related evidence of validity   D. None of the above

7. A high school English teacher, Mrs. Dawson, finds that her state's Board of Education has adopted a set curricular outcomes for each subject area and each grade range in grades K-12. These outcomes are referred to as the state's adopted "Standards of Learning," that is, SOLs. Because Mrs. Dawson believes her mid-semester and semester exams are the most important assessment tools for her to use in determining the quality of her own instruction, she reviews the state's "essential" SOLs for high school English, then carefully decides how many of those SOLs have not been addressed by at least three items in her combined mid-semester and final exams. Happily, she discovers that all but four of the state's "essential" SOLs for high school English have been satisfactorily addressed in her two tests.

    A. Content-related evidence of validity   C. Construct-related evidence of validity
    B. Criterion-related evidence of validity   D. None of the above

8. Erlinda Cruz teaches fifth-graders in a school whose staff has emphasized mathematics instruction as part of its school improvement program. Erlinda has developed an end-of-year mathematics exam that she is confident will identify those students who will succeed or will fail in their middle-school mathematics courses. To verify this belief, she follows as many of her students as she can (those who attend nearby middle schools) to find out what their grades are in any middle-school mathematics course they take. After three years of this follow-up effort, she has solid evidence that her fifth-grade mathematics exam does, indeed, help identify those students who, in middle school, will sail through their math courses or, instead, stumble in those courses.

    A. Content-related evidence of validity   C. Construct-related evidence of validity
    B. Criterion-related evidence of validity   D. None of the above

9. Martin Meadows spends a considerable amount of time making sure that his classroom assessments are as polished as he can make them. To make certain his tests are yielding a relatively unchanging picture of his students' achievements, he routinely re-administers certain of his tests a day or two after they were initially administered. He then correlates each student's first-time score with that same student's second-time score. Because of the care with which Martin devises his tests' items, the relationship between students' first and second performances is typically quite strong and positive.

A. Content-related evidence of validity
B. Criterion-related evidence of validity
C. Construct-related evidence of validity
D. None of the above

10. Floyd Bevins, a fourth grade teacher, wants to make sure that his final examination in science adequately represents the five high-priority science objectives he has chosen for his students. Accordingly, he asks a colleague to review the science examination to make sure that there are enough items on the exam to provide a reasonably accurate estimate of the extent to which each fourth-grader has mastered the science objectives. Floyd's colleague reported that, while four of the five objectives are adequately measured on the exam, one of the objectives seems to be measured by only one item. Moreover, as the colleague exclaimed, "and that was a pretty weak item!

A. Content-related evidence of validity
B. Criterion-related evidence of validity
C. Construct-related evidence of validity
D. None of the above

CHAPTER 4

ABSENCE-OF-BIAS

Instructor to Instructor

Bias Sensitivity: Commercial Tests and Classroom Tests

During the past two decades we have witnessed an enormous expansion in the bias-reduction activities engaged in by the commercial firms that construct/sell nationally standardized tests. Similar bias-reduction activities have been engaged in by the test-development companies that create customized high-stakes tests for states and large school districts. The reason for this intensification of bias-detection zeal is quite simple: fear of litigation.

There are several federal laws now in place that make it possible for citizens (or groups representing them) to successfully sue measurement firms if those agencies have not done a professionally competent job in trying to eliminate assessment bias.

You might wish to note for your students' interest that although NCLB contains many accountability-based assessment requirements, there is nothing in that law calling for the use of NCLB tests in connection with diploma-denial or grade-to-grade promotions. Decisions to use NCLB tests for such purposes are *state* decisions, that is, it is a state's educational policies, not a federal law, that might lead to penalties for individual students. Those are the penalties apt to result in litigation because, for example, a student (U.S. citizen) might have been denied due process as guaranteed by the Constitution. Thus, NCLB, although an immensely important law, is not likely to spur a spate of litigation.

So, 20 years ago we might find a test-development firm giving only token attention to the eradication of bias. Now, for any new tests, there are elaborate judgmental bias reviews undertaken as well as all sorts of empirical bias-detection techniques used (typically referred to as differential item functioning, DIF, bias detection procedure). Test publishers have been burned in court because of insufficient bias-detection efforts. They do not intend to be burned again.

Yet, while there have been dramatic efforts on the part of commercial assessment agencies to get their bias-reduction houses in order, we see almost no attention on the part of classroom teachers to eradicate bias from their own assessments. I find in my own teaching of classroom assessment courses, this is where I need to expand my energy when we tackle the topic of bias.

I really think that most of the experienced teachers who deal with this issue do not believe their tests possess content that would offend or unfairly penalize their students. It is my conviction that they are wrong. I've found the best way to get teachers to realize that their tests may be biased is to put actual tests under rigorous bias-detection scrutiny. (One of the suggested activities for this chapter does just that.) But people typically don't try to repair what they regard as unbroken. So, don't be surprised if you encounter more than a little resistance when teachers talk about their own classroom tests. In my experience, many teachers think that the presence of assessment bias is prevalent in commercial tests, but almost totally absent in teachers' classroom tests. This view, of course, is silly. But it must be adroitly expunged, not pounded out with a mallet. Even seasoned teachers are sensitive to criticism.

Elusive Examples

I've always found it difficult to come up with *acceptable* illustrations of offensive content in test items. For instance, if I describe even an absolutely true story in which a minority person is denigrated, there is the high likelihood that such illustrative denigration will be offensive to some students. If any of my students are members of that minority group, then it is almost certain that those students will be at least uncomfortable and, more likely, offended.

If instructors engage in any illustrative stereotypic put-downs of a group of people, whether it is because of its ethnicity, religion, race, or gender, it is almost certain they'll be disturbing someone. So, I've tried to use more benign examples and hope my students will recognize what I'm trying to get at. It may not always work, but I surely feel more comfortable at the end of the class session than if I had tossed out a stream of on-target but distasteful illustrations.

Activities

There are three suggested activities offered for your consideration based on this chapter. First, students are encouraged to locate an actual classroom test, their own or that of some (other) teacher, then bring it to class for a bias-detection review. If you're working with a group of experienced teachers, this is a fairly simple activity to pull off. If your students are prospective teachers, then it's a good deal more difficult. I suspect that if I were teaching prospective teachers, I'd try to round up actual classroom assessments from real teachers, then hang on to those assessments for use during this sort of activity.

The second activity is intended to have your students recognize there may be instructional benefits derived by isolating the existence of gaps in the performance of minority and majority students on tests whose absence-of-bias has been carefully scrutinized.

The chapter's final activity calls for a whole-class discussion of an often emotionally charged issue, how much assessment accommodation should be made so that disabled students can be more accurately assessed. I have added new material to this chapter based on NCLB's requirements regarding the testing of special-education students and students with limited English proficiency. I hope that those additions will prove helpful.

Chapter Test

A traditional True-False test is provided for this chapter. Actually, I like the sort of bias-detection type of activity seen in the chapter's self-check. However, to provide an overview of the chapter's key content, I think a True-False test does the job reasonably well.

> Answer Key. 1: F, 2: T, 3: F, 4: T, 5: T, 6: F, 7: F, 8: T, 9: T, 10: F.

Chapter Activities

♦♦♦ A Real World Absence-of-Bias Exercise

Give your students a week or so to bring in multiple copies (enough for the class, unless it is too large) of an actual classroom test currently used by a teacher. Then, during a class session, select several of these tests in which you believe there may be biased elements. Split your class into subgroups to review each item using the per-item absence-of-bias review question found in the chapter. After making individual judgments about each item, have each student also review the collectivity of items using the overall absence-of-bias question presented in the chapter. Each subgroup should summarize its per-item and overall absence-of-bias judgments, then be prepared to describe those results to the entire class.

You may wish to use only one or two tests for this activity or, instead, assign a different test to each group. I've tried both approaches and, in my experience, the most insightful class discussions seem to arise when all students have looked at the *same* test.

Post-analysis of these real-world classroom tests almost always leads to my students' identifying serious absence-of-bias deficits with respect to either an item's offensiveness to certain groups or the likelihood that an item would unfairly penalize some students because of group characteristics.

♦♦♦ Deriving Dividends from Disparate Impact

Split your class into groups of two or three, then ask each small group to develop an argument to persuade members of a state board of education a statewide high-stakes test should be used that has (1) successfully passed a rigorous absence-of-bias scrutiny but (2) still has a disparate impact on certain groups of minority students.

Having allowed some time for each group to prepare its argument, then randomly select several groups to deliver their arguments to the rest of the class. The cogency of each group's argument can, after several presentations, be critiqued by the entire class.

♦♦♦ How Accommodating Should Assessment Accommodations Be?

One of the difficult issues to be faced by those who devise assessment accommodations for disabled students is the degree of adjustment that should be made in the assessment procedures. Introduce a total-class discussion of this topic by briefly describing, yourself, the two extremes of most arguments about this issue.

Those in favor of minimal accommodations fear that more meaningful adjustments will lead to significantly different inferences about what achievements a disabled child actually does or doesn't possess. Those in favor of major accommodations contend that a disabled child has already been "dealt an unfortunate hand," hence *any* kind of accommodation is a humane reaction to such disabilities and, therefore, should be permitted.

It is suggested that there be no winners or losers in this discussion. Rather, the purpose of the activity is to let your students see the strength, and often the emotionality, embodied in people's positions regarding this issue—an issue so important to disabled children and their families.

CHAPTER 4 TEST

T   F   1.   If an NCLB test produces a statistically significant disparate impact between minority and majority students' performance, it is certain to possess assessment bias.

T   F   2.   Differential item functioning (DIF) represents today's most common approach to the empirical detection of potentially biased test items.

T   F   3.   For a test item to be biased, it must offend at least one group of students on the basis of group members' personal characteristics such as race, religion, or gender.

T   F   4.   Even if the individual items in a test are judged to be bias-free, it is possible for the total set of items, in aggregate, to be biased.

T   F   5.   Typically, judgment-only approaches to the detection of item bias should be employed prior to use of empirical bias-detection techniques.

T   F   6.   Assessment accommodations require the creation of a substantially new test, hopefully equated to the original test.

T   F   7.   "Limited English Proficient" (LEP) students are those children who have been identified as capable of responding appropriately to an English-language assessment.

T   F   8.   The President's Advisory Commission on Educational Excellence for Hispanic Americans issued a May, 2000 report asserting that state accountability officials "allow Hispanic youngsters to become invisible inside the very system charged with educating them."

T   F   9.   If a teacher's classroom test in mathematics dealt with content more likely to be familiar to girls than boys, it is likely that the test may be biased.

T   F   10.   Empirical bias-detection techniques, especially DIF-biased approaches, will invariably identify more biased items than will even a well-trained and representative bias-review committee.

CHAPTER 5

DECIDING WHAT TO ASSESS AND HOW TO ASSESS IT

Instructor to Instructor

Separate Empires

For over ten years, I headed a test-development group that created high-stakes achievement tests for a dozen states and several large school districts. During these typically lengthy test-development projects, I discovered a profound truth regarding the educators with whom I was collaborating. Whether at the state or district level, the measurement people rarely worked with the curriculum people, and the curriculum folks rarely worked with their assessment counterparts. Moreover, I often witnessed hostility between members of the curriculum and assessment camps.

After seeing this antipathy between measurement specialists and curriculum specialists, I concluded that the chief cause for this often hostility was simply ignorance. The assessment people, not really understanding the innards of curriculum and instruction, typically denigrated that which they did not understand. And the curriculum folks were usually intimidated by anyone who comfortably say that a test had "a Cronbach *Alpha* coefficient of only .44."

Well, perhaps there was a time for such a separate-enclaves approach to education, but that time has disappeared. These days, with so much impact of high-stakes testing on what teachers teach, it is imperative that curriculum and assessment specialists learn enough about the other person's game so that, at least in a rudimentary way, they can play it. This chapter, focused mostly on curricular questions, gives you a chance to stress the importance of a teacher's understanding of both curriculum and instruction.

A Team-Teaching Delight

Years ago, when I taught at San Francisco State University, our faculty voted to have the staff provide most of our courses via teaching teams composed of two or three faculty members. Being a docile (and untenured) faculty member, I readily complied.

I hated it. My team members and I spent so much time in the planning of our upcoming classes that, after hours of negotiation, I was almost too exhausted to teach. I left that two years of team turmoil convinced that I'd never teach-team again. And yet I did.

The last five years I was at UCLA, before taking early retirement in 1991 (largely because emeritus faculty received free campus-parking), I team-taught a course with Madeline Hunter of the UCLA faculty. Our course focused on the relationship between educational testing and teaching. It was a joy—one of the best teaching experiences I had at UCLA. Madeline was, before her death several years later, the most active and, I believe, most influential staff developer in the nation. She knew how to help experienced teachers come up with instructional insights that they could use the very next day they taught. Our field is less potent because of her loss.

Well, at any rate, Madeline's students knew lots about curriculum and instruction, but almost nothing about assessment. My students, on the other hand, possessed a pile of measurement moxie, but most would have been challenged if they had been called on to whip up a winning lesson plan.

But the interchanges among our students were marvelous. Each group learned, I believe, to recognize that a potent educational professional needs to understand *both* curriculum and assessment. If you agree, then this chapter provides an opportunity for you to advocate that sort of stance.

Activities

Consistent with the view that teachers need to become skilled in dealing with both assessment and curriculum, in the next few pages you'll find two somewhat lengthy excerpts from the curriculum/assessment frameworks devised for the civics and mathematics tests of the National Assessment of Educational Progress (NAEP). NAEP is briefly described in this chapter of *Classroom Assessment*. There are many ways that you can use these materials for meaningful dips into the linkage between assessment and curriculum. Two possible activities are described for your consideration, but I suspect you can come up with even better ones. Simply photocopy the relevant pages (choosing from civics or mathematics), then get your students to employ some of Chapter 5's concepts in dealing with either or both of those frameworks. The big challenge for teachers is coping with far too many content standards (that is, curricular aims). This chapter tries to lay out the options for teachers who find that there are too many content standards supposedly measured by their state's NCLB tests. If such is the situation in the state where your students are (or will be) teaching, a discussion of this issue should prove beneficial.

Chapter Test

The test for Chapter 5 taps lightly on the same sort of content addressed in the chapter's Self-Check, but does so in the form of short-answer items. These items are absolutely *short*-answer items because, as you will see, the student's response is limited to no more than *seven* words.

Answer Key. 1: Broad-scope Objective, 2: Broad-scope Objective, 3: There is no significant difference., 4: Too numerous or too general, 5: Affective, 6: There is considerable disagreement among educators regarding the meaning of "alignment" largely because of variations in the stringency required for genuine alignment, 7: Because without an identification of the most important content standards, there are typically too many content standards to teach or to test in the time available, 8: State NCLB performance standards are likely to be set at lower levels of rigor than NAEP performance standards because, if the two sets of standards were identical, too many students would fail to be classified as "proficient" on state NCLB tests, 9: It is the inference, not the test, that is norm- or criterion-referenced., 10: Cognitive—and usually at the lowest level.

Chapter Activities

In the next several pages, you will find excerpts from two of the NAEP assessment frameworks. The first is an appendix drawn from the 1998 NAEP Civics Framework.* This framework is structured around (1) *organizing questions and content summaries*, (2) *intellectual skills*, (3) *participatory skills*, and (4) *civics dispositions*. The content for the five organizing questions is set forth for grades 4, 8, and 12. The intellectual skills, participatory skills, and civic dispositions are not categorized according to grade levels. The second NAEP framework is excerpted from the 1996 and 2000 assessment framework.* There are five content strands for the framework, namely, (1) number sense, properties, and operations; (2) measurement; (3) geometry and spatial sense; (4) analysis, statistics, and probability; and (5) algebra and functions. Because of space limitations, and the ease of usage in class activities, I have included the introductory material for all five content strands, but only the framework for the first content strand, that is, number sense, properties, and operations. As you will see, the NAEP Mathematics Framework is set up differently than the NAEP Civics Framework. Nevertheless, in both frameworks there are identifications of the topics and subtopics eligible to be included in the actual NAEP assessments at grades 4, 8, and 12.

♦♦♦ Categorizing Content

One possible activity you might consider is to duplicate one or both of the NAEP frameworks, then ask your students to classify segments of the content using any of the categorization schemes described in the chapter, for example, broad-scope versus small-scope objectives. You might also ask your students to designate, for certain content in the frameworks, whether a selected-response or constructed-response assessment strategy would lead to tests from which more valid inferences would be derivative. In short, use any of the chapter's concepts to have your students work with the *curricular* content seen in these frameworks.

♦♦♦ Prioritizing Import

Educators want to teach everything and to test everything. Yet, given finite teaching time and limited testing time, choices must be made. You might split your students into subgroups, then isolate a specific section of one of the frameworks, and ask the students to rank-order the five (or some number of your choice) most important things to be assessed. Get them to realize that they typically can't "measure it all." So, via individual and then pooled rankings, see if there are any between-group disparities in the resultant rankings.

---

* U.S. Department of Education. (No Date). *Civics Framework for the 1998 National Assessment of Educational Progress: NAEP Civics Consensus Project* (NAGB Contract ZA95001001).
* U.S. Department of Education. (No Date). *Mathematics Framework for the 1996 and 2000 National Assessment of Educational Progress: NAEP Mathematics Consensus Project* (NAGB Contract RN 91084001).

AN EXCERPT FROM THE CIVICS FRAMEWORK FOR THE 1998 NATIONAL ASSESSMENT OF EDUCATIONAL PROGRESS

Structured According To:

- **Organizing Questions and Content Summaries**
- **Intellectual Skills**
- **Participatory Skills**
- **Civic Dispositions**

Civic Dispositions

As used in this document, the term "Assessment Framework" means the content and overall design that have been developed in the consensus building process to guide the preparation of the 1998 Civics Assessment. The term "Framework document" means this document—the text in which the Framework, as created in the consensus building process, is contained. The term "standards" refers to criteria that should guide civic education in the schools and by which assessments of students' achievement could be made.

In the 1998 Assessment Framework, the term "citizen" will be used in a broad, encompassing sense. For example, students are citizens of their classroom and their school. They also are citizens of their neighborhood and community. The term citizenship also is used more precisely where it is appropriate to do so, to refer to natural-born and naturalized "citizens of the United States and of the state wherein they reside."

The term "Americans" also is used throughout this Framework. While it is true that others in the Western Hemisphere also consider themselves to be "Americans," that name generally is recognized as designating the people of the United States of America.

NAEP Civics Assessment
Organizing Questions and Content Summary for: Part I

I. What Are Civic Life, Politics, and Government?		
Grade 4	**Grade 8**	**Grade 12**
Definition of government Difference between power, authority Necessity, purposes of government: • Make, carry out, enforce laws. • Manage conflicts. • Provide for the defense of the nation. Importance of rules, laws: • Purposes of rules, laws. • Evaluating rules, laws. Major difference between limited government, unlimited government	Definition of civic life, politics, government, civil society Difference between power, authority Necessity, purposes of politics, government Limited, unlimited governments The rule of law Purposes, uses of constitutions Conditions under which constitutional government flourishes Alternative ways of organizing constitutional governments: • Shared powers, parliamentary systems. • Confederal, federal, unitary systems.	Definition of civic life, politics, constitutional government, civil society Difference between power, authority Necessity, purposes of politics, government Limited unlimited governments The rule of law Civil society, limited government Relationship of limited government to political, economic freedom Purposes, uses of constitutions Conditions under which constitutional government flourishes Alternative ways of organizing constitutional governments: • Shared powers, parliamentary systems. • Confederal, federal, unitary systems. Obligations of representatives in constitutional governments

NAEP Civics Assessment
Organizing Questions and Content Summary for: Part II

II. What Are the Foundations of the American Political System?		
Grade 4	**Grade 8**	**Grade 12**
Fundamental values, principles	American idea of constitutional government	American idea of constitutional government
Distinctive characteristics of American society	Distinctive characteristics of American society	Distinctive characteristics of American society
Unity, diversity in American society: • Ideals of American democracy. • American identity. • Costs, benefits of unity, diversity.	Role of voluntarism in American life	Role of voluntarism in American life
	Unity, diversity in American society	Role of organized groups in political life
Prevention and management of conflicts	Character of American political conflict	Unity, diversity in American society
	Fundamental values, principles of American constitutional democracy	Character of American political conflict
	Conflicts among values, principles in American political, social life	Influence of classical liberalism, republicanism on American constitutional democracy
	Disparities between ideals, reality in American political, social life	Fundamental values, principles of American constitutional democracy
		Conflicts among values, principles in American political, social life
		Disparities between ideals, reality in American political, social life

NAEP Civics Assessment
Organizing Questions and Content Summary for: Part III

III. How Does the Government Established by the Constitution Embody the Purposes, Values, and Principles of American Democracy?		
Grade 4	**Grade 8**	**Grade 12**
Meaning, importance of the U.S. constitution	Distributing, sharing, limiting powers of the national government	Distributing governmental power, preventing its abuse
Major responsibilities, services of state governments	Major responsibilities of national government for domestic, foreign policy	Major responsibilities of the national government:
Major responsibilities, services of local governments	The federal system	Constitutional status, major responsibilities of state, local governments
Key leaders in local, state, national governments	Organization, major responsibilities of state, local governments	Financing government through taxation
Contacting public officials, agencies	Financing government through taxation	Law in American society, protection of individual rights
	Law in American society	The public agenda
	Political communication	Political communication: television, radio, press, political persuasion
	Political parties, interest groups, campaigns	Political parties, interest groups, campaigns, elections
	Voting, elections	Public opinion, behavior of the electorate
	Civil society: nongovernmental associations, groups	Civil society: nongovernmental associations, groups
	Forming, carrying out public policy	Forming, carrying out public policy
	Leaders in local, state, national governments: how to monitor, influence them	Leaders in local, state, national governments: how to monitor, influence them

NAEP Civics Assessment
Organizing Questions and Content Summary for: Part IV

IV. What is the Relationship of the United States to Other Nations and to World Affairs?		
Grade 4	**Grade 8**	**Grade 12**
The concept of nation	Nation-states	Nation-states
Interaction among nations: • Trade. • Diplomacy. • Cultural context. • Treaties and agreements. • Military force.	Interaction among nation-states	Interaction among nation-states
	U.S. relations with other nation-states	The breakdown of order among nation-states
Importance of peaceful resolution of international conflicts	Major governmental, non-governmental international organizations	Making, implementing U.S. foreign policy
		Ends and means of U.S. foreign policy
	Impact of the American concept of democracy, individual rights on the world	Major foreign policy positions of the United States
	The influence of other nations on American politics, society	The influence of other nations on American politics, society
	Effects of significant world political, demographic, environmental developments, and trends on the United States	Impact of the American concept of democracy, individual rights on the world
		Effects of significant world political, demographic, environmental developments, trends on the United States
		United States, major governmental and nongovernmental international organizations

NAEP Civics Assessment
Organizing Questions and Content Summary for: Part V

V. What Are the Roles of Citizens in American Democracy?		
Grade 4	**Grade 8**	**Grade 12**
Meaning of citizenship; becoming a citizen	Difference between a subject and a citizen	Meaning of citizenship; becoming a citizen
Important rights of citizens	Meaning of citizenship; becoming a citizen	Personal, political, economic rights
Personal, civic responsibilities	Personal, political, economic rights	Relationships among personal, political, economic rights
Civic dispositions that foster: • Individual independence. • Respect for human dignity. • Assumption of personal, political, economic responsibilities. • Participation in civic affairs. • Healthy functioning of American constitutional democracy.	Scope, limits of rights Personal, civic responsibilities Civic dispositions that foster: • Individual independence. • Respect for human dignity. • Assumption of personal, political, economic responsibilities. • Participation in civic affairs. • Healthy functioning of American constitutional democracy.	Scope, limits of rights Personal, civic responsibilities Relationship between politics and the attainment of individual and public goals Difference between political and social participation Civic dispositions that foster: • Individual independence. • Respect for human dignity. • Assumption of personal, political, economic responsibilities. • Participation in civic affairs. • Healthy functioning of American constitutional democracy.
Opportunities for civic participation: • Discussing public issues. • Communicating with public officials and agencies. • Voting. • Attending meetings of governing bodies. Criteria for selecting leaders Importance of political leadership, public service	Opportunities for civic participation Criteria for selecting leaders Importance of political leadership, public service	Opportunities for civic participation Criteria for selecting leaders Importance of political leadership, public service

31

NAEP Civics Assessment: Intellectual Skills

Identifying and Describing	Explaining and Analyzing	Evaluating, Taking, and Defending a Position
• Defining key terms.	• Explaining how something works.	• Identifying strengths, weaknesses.
• Making distinctions.	• Explaining causes, effects of events, phenomena.	• Challenging *ad hominem* arguments.
• Identifying individuals, symbols, institutions.	• Comparing, contrasting.	• Questioning the validity of arguments, data, analogies.
• Identifying ideas, concepts.	• Analyzing reasons for acts, occurrences, trends.	• Citing evidence in support or rejection of ideas, positions.
• Identifying emotional language, symbols.	• Distinguishing between fact and opinion.	• Predicting probable consequences.
• Describing functions and processes.	• Distinguishing between means and ends.	• Critiquing means, ends.
• Determining origins.	• Clarifying meaning, relationships.	• Assessing costs, benefits of alternatives.
• Describing attributes, characteristics.	• Clarifying responsibilities.	• Choosing a position from existing alternatives.
• Classifying by attributes.	• Interpreting the meaning or significance of events, ideas, phenomena.	• Creating a novel position.
• Describing trends.		• Defending a position.
		• Responding to opposing arguments.

NAEP Civics Assessment: Participatory Skills

Interacting	Monitoring	Influencing
• Working in small groups, committees.	• Discussing public affairs.	• Voting.
• Listening.	• Tracking public issues in the media.	• Representing one's own or a group's interest.
• Questioning to clarify information, points of view.	• Researching public issues.	• Petitioning.
• Discussing public affairs.	• Gathering information from government officials and agencies, interest groups, civic organizations.	• Writing letters, op-ed pieces, broadsides, pamphlets.
• Participating in civic, interest groups.		• Speaking, testifying before public bodies.
• Building coalitions, enlisting support of other like-minded groups.	• Attending public meetings and hearings.	• Participating in civic organizations, political parties, interest groups.
• Managing conflicts: mediating, negotiating, compromising, seeking consensus, adjudicating.	• Interviewing people knowledgeable about civic issues.	• Supporting and opposing candidates or positions on public issues.
• Performing school and community service, serving as a representative or elected leader.	• Questioning public officials, experts, others to elicit information, fix responsibility.	• Using computer networks to advance points of view on public affairs.
• Using print and electronic resources to acquire, exchange information.	• Using print and electronic resources to acquire, exchange information.	

NAEP Civics Assessment: Civic Dispositions

Civic dispositions or traits of private and public character important to the preservation and improvement of American constitutional democracy:

- Becoming an independent member of society.

- Respecting individual worth and human dignity.

- Assuming the personal, political, and economic responsibilities of a citizen.

- Participating in civic affairs in an informed, thoughtful, and effective manner.

- Promoting the healthy functioning of American constitutional democracy.

AN EXCERPT FROM THE MATHEMATICS FRAMEWORK FOR THE 1996 AND 2000 NATIONAL ASSESSMENT OF EDUCATIONAL PROGRESS

- **An introduction for all five content strands, namely, (1) number sense, properties, and operations; (2) measurement; (3) geometry and spatial sense; (4) analysis, statistics, and probability; and (5) algebra and functions**

- **The NAEP framework for number sense, properties, and operations**

1996 and 2000 NAEP Mathematics Objectives

Mathematical Content Areas and Assessment Strands

To conduct a meaningful assessment of mathematics proficiency, it is necessary to measure students' proficiencies in various content areas. As in the 1990 and 1992 assessments, five mathematical strands will be used to categorize mathematical content for the 1996 and 2000 mathematics assessments. The strands are illustrated later in this chapter. Classification of topics into these strands cannot be exact, however, and inevitably will involve some overlap. For example, some topics appearing under data analysis, statistics, and probability may be closely related to others that appear under algebra and functions. As assessment programs continue to be refined, it becomes less desirable to force every item into only one content description category. Students are expected to solve problems that naturally involve more than one specific mathematical topic. Consequently, the assessment as a whole will address the topics and subtopics identified in this chapter, and every item will be categorized under primarily one topic and subtopic so that analysis of results may be somewhat specific. Ideally, however, the items will involve students in synthesizing knowledge across topics and subtopics, and occasionally it may be difficult to identify a unique topic for each item. In fact, it is desirable that at least half of the new items for the assessment should involve content from more than one topic, or even from more than one strand.

The following sections of this chapter provide a brief description of each content strand with a list of topics and subtopics illustrative of those to be included in the assessment. This level of specificity is needed to guide item writers and ensure adequate coverage of the content areas and abilities to be assessed. The five content strands are largely consistent with the strands used in the 1990 and 1992 assessments. The titles and emphases of the content areas have been modified to reflect more clearly the directions for curriculum and evaluation described in the NCTM *Standards*.

For each grade (4, 8, and 12), the following symbols are used: a "•" indicates that the subtopic could be assessed at that grade level, a "△" indicates that the subtopic should not be assessed at that grade level, and a "#" indicates that the subtopic might be introduced in the assessment at a very simple level, probably using a manipulative or pictorial model. The test specifications include additional detail and descriptions of how item types, families, calculators, manipulatives, and special studies fit within and across topics and subtopics.

Number Sense, Properties, and Operations

This strand focuses on students' understanding of numbers (whole numbers, fractions, decimals, integers, real numbers, and complex numbers), operations, and estimation, and their application to real-world situations. Students will be expected to demonstrate an understanding of numerical relationships as expressed in ratios, proportions, and percentages. Students also will be expected to understand properties of numbers and operations, generalize from numerical patterns, and verify results.

Number sense includes items that address a student's understanding of relative size, equivalent forms of numbers, and his or her use of numbers to represent attributes of real-world objects and quantities. Items that call for students to complete open sentences involving basic number facts are considered part of this content area. Items that require some application of the definition of operations and related procedures are classified under the area of algebra and functions.

The emphasis in computation is on understanding when to use an operation, knowing what the operation means, and being able to estimate and use mental techniques in addition to performing calculations using computational algorithms. In terms of actual computation, students will be expected to demonstrate that they know how to perform basic algorithms and use calculators in appropriate ways, given more complex situations. While a few isolated computation items may be included, a priority will be placed on including items in which operations are used in meaningful contexts.

The grade 4 assessment will emphasize the development of number sense through the connection of a variety of models to their numerical representations, as well as emphasizing an understanding of the meaning of addition, subtraction, multiplication, and division. These concepts will be addressed for whole numbers, simple fractions, and decimals at this grade level, with continual emphasis on the use of models and their connection to the use of symbols.

The grade 8 assessment will include number sense extended to include both positive and negative numbers and will address properties and operations involving whole numbers, fractions, decimals, integers, and rational numbers. The use of ratios and proportional thinking to represent situations involving quantity is a major focus at this grade level, and students will be expected to know how to read, use, and apply scientific notation to represent large and small numbers.

At grade 12, the assessment will include both real and complex numbers and will allow students to demonstrate competency through approximately the precalculus or calculus level. Operations with powers and roots, as well as a variety of real and complex numbers, may be assessed. Including a broad range of items at this level will ensure that students who have had different types of high school mathematics courses will be able to demonstrate proficiency in some parts of this content area.

NAEP Mathematics Content Strand 1

		Grade	
Number Sense, Properties, and Operations	**4**	**8**	**12**

1. Relate counting, grouping, and place value

   a. Use place value to model and describe whole numbers and decimals   •   •   •

   b. Use scientific notation in meaningful contexts   Δ   •   •

> • Subtopic can be assessed at this grade level.
> Δ Subtopic should not be assessed at this grade level.
> # Subtopic may be introduced at a simple level (such as using a manipulative or pictorial model).

		Grade	
Number Sense, Properties, and Operations	**4**	**8**	**12**

2. Represent numbers and operations in a variety of equivalent forms using models, diagrams, and symbols

   a. Model numbers using set models such as counters — • △ △

   b. Model numbers using number lines — • • △

   c. Use two- and three-dimensional region models to describe numbers — • • •

   d. Use other models appropriate to a given situation (for example, draw diagrams to represent a number or an operation; write a number sentence to fit a situation or describe a situation to fit a number sentence; interpret calculator or computer displays) — • • •

   e. Read, write, rename, order, and compare numbers — • • •

3. Compute with numbers (that is, add, subtract, multiply, divide)

   a. Apply basic properties of operations — • • •

   b. Describe effect of operations on size and order of numbers — • • •

   c. Describe features of algorithms (such as regrouping with or without manipulatives, partial products) — • • •

   d. Select appropriate computation method (such as pencil and paper, calculator, mental arithmetic) — • • •

4. Use computation and estimation in applications

   a. Round whole numbers, decimals, and fractions in meaningful contexts — • • •

   b. Make estimates appropriate to a given situation

     i. Know when to estimate — • • •

     ii. Select appropriate type of estimate (overestimate, underestimate, range of estimate) — • • •

     iii. Describe order of magnitude (estimation related to place value, scientific notation) — • • •

   c. Select appropriate method of estimation (such as front end, rounding) — • • •

   d. Solve application problems involving numbers and operations using exact answers or estimates as appropriate — • • •

   e. Interpret round-off errors using calculators/computers (that is, truncating) — △ # •

• Subtopic can be assessed at this grade level.
△ Subtopic should not be assessed at this grade level.
\# Subtopic may be introduced at a simple level (such as using a manipulative or pictorial model).

Number Sense, Properties, and Operations	Grade		
	4	8	12

   f. Verify solutions and determine the reasonableness of results

      i. In real-world situations   ●   ●   ●

      ii. In abstract settings   Δ   Δ   ●

5. Apply ratios and proportional thinking in a variety of situations

   a. Use ratios to describe situations   #   ●   ●

   b. Use proportions to model problems   Δ   ●   ●

   c. Use proportional thinking to solve problems (including rates, scaling, and similarity)   Δ   ●   ●

   d. Understand the meaning of percentage (including percentages greater than 100 and less than 1)   #   ●   ●

   e. Solve problems involving percentages   Δ   ●   ●

6. Use elementary number theory

   a. Describe odd and even numbers and their characteristics   ●   ●   ●

   b. Describe number patterns   #   ●   ●

   c. Use factors and multiples to model and solve problems   Δ   ●   ●

   d. Describe prime numbers   Δ   ●   ●

   e. Use divisibility and remainders in problem settings (including simple modular arithmetic)   Δ   #   ●

● Subtopic can be assessed at this grade level.
Δ Subtopic should not be assessed at this grade level.
Subtopic may be introduced at a simple level (such as using a manipulative or pictorial model).

CHAPTER 5 TEST

Directions: Respond to each of the short-answer items in this test by using *no more than seven words* in a response.

1. Here's an instructional objective: "Students will become conversant with the pivotal political events underlying the initiation of the Civil War." Is this a small-scope objective or a broad-scope objective?

    _____

2. Consider the following instructional objective: "At the end of the 10-week unit on narrative writing, students will be able to write an acceptable narrative essay on any assigned topic dealing with an historical event with which they are familiar." Is this a small-scope objective or a broad-scope objective?

    _____

3. What is the significant difference, if any, between an "instructional objective" and a "content standard?"

    _____

4. Most current sets of content standards suffer from one or more serious shortcomings. What is *one* of those deficiencies?

    _____

5. Here's an instructional objective: "Students will develop a discernible disposition to learn more, that is, a positive attitude toward the learning process itself." Using Bloom's Taxonomy, should you classify this objective as affective, psychomotor, or cognitive?

    _____

6. Is there substantial agreement among educators regarding the concept of "alignment" between curriculum and assessment? If so, what is the agreed meaning? If not, why is there disagreement regarding this concept?

_____

7. In the Chapter it was recommended that content standards be *prioritized*. Why?

_____

8. NAEP tests are reported in for categories, that is, *advanced, proficient, basic,* and *below basic.* According to NCLB, states are permitted to set their own performance standards (that is, their own "student academic achievement standards"). Is it likely that most state's NCLB performance standards will coincide with level of rigor embodied in the NAEP performance standards? Why or why not?

_____

9. Why is it technically inaccurate to refer to a "criterion-referenced test" or a "norm-referenced test?"

_____

10. Using Bloom's Taxonomy, what kinds of instructional objectives are most frequently measured by teachers' classroom assessments?

_____

CHAPTER 6

SELECTED-RESPONSE TESTS

Instructor to Instructor

And Now For Something Completely Practical

It never ceases to amaze me that most experienced teachers who take a classroom assessment workshop from me almost always get excited when we start dealing with the nuts and bolts of various item types. I personally get much more enthused about issues related to validity, absence-of-bias, and determining what a teacher ought to be measuring. So I routinely assume that seasoned teachers will share my enthusiasms. More often than not, they don't.

But they do get turned on by chapters such as this one and the several that follow it. What's going on, I suspect, is that these teachers enjoy acquiring a set of *tangible skills* about how to create the various sorts of test items that they can use in the creation of their own classroom assessments. There's something so down-to-earth about a set of dos and don'ts for writing different types of items. I guess, after years of tussling with innards of a true-false item, I just can't get all that excited by six item-writing guidelines for the birthing of binary-choice items. But, when teachers wander out the door after dealing with this chapter's contents, they often indicate how "interesting that stuff was." I no longer become amazed, only a mite amused. I have, it appears, become jaded about the joys of ginning up various species of practical, real world test items.

Practice and Perfection

Clearly, the more practice that you can give your own students in creating items that cleave to this chapter's mandates regarding item-construction, the better. In my own classes, I've been able to rely heavily on the kinds of chapter-related activities you'll be reading about shortly. The only occasion when I can't rely on such peer-critiquing kinds of exercises is when I have to cram too much content into a workshop that's only scheduled for a few days. Skinny workshops leave little room for "practice makes perfect." In some cases, indeed, practice in item-writing is far less abundant than, I am sure, is necessary. I hope you have ample time to sharpen your own students' item-writing skills with oodles of time-on-task practice.

Activities

Based on the previous paragraph, you should not be surprised to learn that all three of the *IRM*'s potential activities for Chapter 6 focus on students' creating and critiquing selected-response test items.

Chapter Test

The chapter test presents a set of selected-response test items, each of which contains one dominant shortcoming, that is, a violation of *one* of the five general item-writing commandments given early in the chapter or a violation of *one* of the item-writing guidelines supplied in the chapter for the particular kind of item presented in the chapter test. Students are to *construct* their answers regarding the defects of the test's *selected*-response items. (Just a smidge of schizophrenia shouldn't hurt all that much!)

<u>Answer Key</u>. (Because flawed items sometimes incorporate multiple shortcomings, I have tried to identify every item's *chief* problem. If you find others that you and your students regard as important, feel free to expand this answer key.) 1: This is a double-concept item., 2: The use of the article "an" renders only Choice C a grammatically correct option., 3: This item maximizes, not minimizes negatives., 4: The dreaded "All of the above" was used., 5: The responses are not ordered logically., 6: This item's stem is too terse and its alternatives too verbose., 7: This item is ambiguous because it is unclear to whom the pronoun "they" refers, that is, to the "teachers" or the "students" in the statement., 8: This item violates the commandment to which it refers by using excessively advanced vocabulary terms., 9: This item violates the guideline urging the avoidance of negatives in a multiple-choice item's stem. If a negative is employed, it should certainly be clearly identified rather than hiding it as an *unitalicized* contracted form of "is not.", 10: This item royally violates the item-writing commandment about the avoidance of complex syntax.

Chapter Activities

♦♦♦ Item Swapping

Divide your class into subgroups, then ask each group to create a number of selected-response items. (You choose the number that best meshes with your available time. I often get the groups to construct five or six items). At least *some* of the items should *dominantly* violate one of the chapter's five general item-writing commandments or the specific item-writing guidelines associated with the item-type (binary choice, for example) the group has constructed. (Some items, therefore, may be unflawed.)

Then, after all groups have created their sometimes-flawed set of items, have groups exchange their item-sets to see if students other than the items' progenitors can spot an item's shortcomings. Disagreements can be resolved by you or by class discussion.

♦♦♦ Transparent Errors

If you have access to an overhead projector and a supply of blank transparencies and suitable marking pens, split your class into groups of two or three students, then ask each group to prepare a selected-response item that is either unflawed *or* flawed because of one chief shortcoming. Then, the items having been constructed, get students to display the items using the overhead projector. Get the rest of the class to register, via a raised-hand vote, whether the item shown is flawless or flawed. If it is determined to be flawed, see if students can spot the item's chief shortcoming.

◆◆◆ Real-World Tests

Given your circumstances, see if there's any way your students can borrow (from a current teacher) a classroom test in which there are a substantial number of selected-response items. Then make photocopies of one or more of these tests that you have pre-screened (so that the class will be able to see some rule-violations!). Then, as a total group or in subgroups, go through these real-world tests to see if there are any of the defects identified in the chapter.

CHAPTER 6 TEST

Directions: Each of the following items is based on a flawed selected-response test item. There will be one *dominant* deficit in each item. The deficits will reflect violations either of the chapter's five general item-writing commandments or of the item-writing guidelines associated with the type of selected-response item presented. You are to identify each item's dominant shortcoming in the space provided.

1. • True? or False? A classroom test that measures appropriate knowledge and/or skills is likely to be reliable because of the strong link between validity and reliability.

   What is this item's dominant shortcoming?

   _____

   _____

2. • If a classroom teacher actually computed a Kuder-Richardson coefficient for a final exam, this would be an example of an:

   A. stability reliability coefficient

   B. internal consistency reliability coefficient

   C. content validity coefficient

   D. construct validity coefficient

   What is this item's dominant shortcoming?

   _____

   _____

3. • True? or False? Test items should never be constructed that fail to display a decisive absence of elements that would have a negative impact on students because of their gender or ethnicity.

   What is this item's dominant shortcoming?

   _____

   _____

4.

> • Which of the following men was a U.S. president during the twentieth century?
>
>   A. Franklin Roosevelt
>
>   B. Jimmy Carter
>
>   C. Dwight Eisenhower
>
>   D. All of the above

What is this item's dominant shortcoming?

_____

_____

5.

> • Directions: On the line to the left of each state in Column A write the letter of the city from the list in Column B that is the state's capitol. Each city in Column B can be used only once.
>
> | Column A | Column B |
> |---|---|
> | _____ 1. Oregon | a. Bismarck |
> | _____ 2. Florida | b. Tallahassee |
> | _____ 3. California | c. Los Angeles |
> | _____ 4. Washington | d. Salem |
> | _____ 5. Kansas | e. Topeka |
> | | f. Sacramento |
> | | g. Olympia |
> | | h. Seattle |

What is this item's dominant shortcoming?

_____

_____

6.

> - A set of properly constructed binary-choice items will:
>
>   A. typically contain a substantially greater proportion of items representing one of the two alternatives available to examinees.
>
>   B. incorporate qualities that permit examinees to immediately recognize the category into which each item falls, even based on only superficial analyses.
>
>   C. vary the length of items representing each of the two binary-option categories so that, without exception, shorter items represent one category while longer items represent the other.
>
>   D. contain no items in which more than a single concept is incorporated in each of the items.

What is this item's dominant shortcoming?

_____

_____

7.

> - Correct? or Incorrect? When teachers assess their students, it is imperative that they understand the content standard on which the test is based.

What is this item's dominant shortcoming?

_____

_____

8.

> - True? or False? One of the most heinous transgressions in the genesis of assessment items is the item's incorporation of obfuscative verbiage.

What is this item's dominant shortcoming?

_____

_____

9.
> - Which of the following isn't an example of how one might collect construct-related evidence of validity?
>
>   A. intervention studies
>   B. test-retest studies
>   C. differential-population studies
>   D. related-measures studies

What is this item's dominant shortcoming?

_____

_____

10.
> - <u>True? or False?</u> Having undertaken a variety of proactive steps to forestall the inclusion of items that might, due to an item's content, have an unwarrantedly adverse impact on students because of any student's personal characteristics, the test-developers then, based on sound methodological guidelines, should carry out a series of empirically based bias-detection studies.

What is this item's dominant shortcoming?

_____

_____

CHAPTER 7

CONSTRUCTED-RESPONSE TESTS

Instructor to Instructor

Patience, Partners

At the beginning of Chapter 7, I spend a few paragraphs trying to explain to readers why I split off the performance assessment chapter (Chapter 8) from this one. My wife would probably say, as she often says about so many of my explanations, "That's the guilty speaking first!" In this instance, I suspect she's correct because the material in Chapter 8 dealing with rubrics is so clearly pertinent to Chapter 7's dip into constructed-response testing.

Nevertheless, when I teach a classroom assessment course, I'll probably continue to split performance assessment from constructed-response assessment just because, if combined, they represent an excessively large chunk of information. But I surely would like my students to understand the innards of rubrics by the time they're really into the scoring of students' responses to essay tests. Actually, sometime I'd like to try having my students read Chapter 7 *and* the nine or so pages in Chapter 8 dealing with rubrics. I've not done so in the past. It might work or, as is often the case, it might not. If you get the urge to try it, and it turns out well, let me know (wpopham@ucla.edu). You can even let me know if it flops!

Activities

Two possible activities are presented for this chapter. The first asks students to prepare an oral presentation about the building and scoring of essay tests. The second deals with a mock debate regarding the competing virtues of constructed-response versus selected-response items.

Chapter Test

Because many of the important admonitions offered in the chapter do not lend themselves readily to concise assessment, I have elected to employ a binary-choice approach to assess students' familiarity with four sets of Chapter 7 mandates, namely, (1) item-writing guidelines for short-answer items, (2) item-writing guidelines for essay items, (3) guidelines for scoring responses to essay items and, because they definitely apply to this chapter's items, (4) the five general item-writing commandments introduced in Chapter 6.

> Answer Key. 1: I, 2: I, 3: A, 4: I, 5: A, 6: A, 7: A, 8: I, 9: I, 10: I, 11: A, 12: I, 13: A, 14: I, 15: I.

Chapter Activities

♦♦♦ A Staff-Development Presentation

After dividing your class into subgroups, each of which is assigned a number, explain that in the next 15-20 minutes, each group is to prepare an oral presentation that could be made at a school-level faculty meeting as part of a staff-development session regarding how best to create and use essay tests. Each subgroup is to prepare an oral presentation of approximately 10-15 minutes duration regarding "Essay Tests: How to Build Them and How to Score Them." The presentation can be made by one or more members of a subgroup. Indicate that, after the subgroups have been given sufficient time, one subgroup will be selected at random to make its presentation to the rest of the class who, at that point, are to assume the role of teachers at a school staff-development session.

Using numbers on slips of paper, have one of your students select the "winning" subgroup whose members, then, make their oral presentation. At the close of the presentation, a total class discussion of the presentation's strengths and weaknesses can conclude the activity.

♦♦♦ Mini-Debates Over Item Types

Split your class into two-person teams. Ask each person to prepare for a brief oral presentation in defense of the proposition that "Selected-response items are better for classroom tests than constructed-response items." This can be labeled Proposition S (for selected-response). Give them five minutes to do so. (They can make notes from which to speak if they wish.) As soon as they have done this, tell them to immediately plan a brief oral presentation on the other side of the issue, namely, "Constructed-response items are better for classroom tests than selected-response items." This can be labeled Proposition C (for constructed-response). Again, allow five minutes for students to organize their thinking.

At that point, using a coin flip, each pair should decide which person will go first in a brief oral mini-debate about item types. Thereupon, a second coin flip will decide whether the first speaker begins by defending Proposition S or Proposition C. As soon as the first of the two speakers is finished, the second member of the pair defends the other proposition.

After all mini-debates have been concluded, a general class discussion should be held to see if there are, in reality—not pretense, any strong supporters of either proposition. Reasons for such advocacy should be examined by the class.

CHAPTER 7 TEST

> Directions: Please read each of the statements presented below, then signify whether the statement is Accurate (Circle the A.) or Inaccurate (Circle the I.). A statement's accuracy depends on whether it represents a verbatim or appropriately paraphrased rendition of statements drawn from Chapter 7's (1) item-writing guidelines for short-answer items, (2) item-writing guidelines for essay items, (3) guidelines for scoring responses to essay items and, from Chapter 6, (4) the five general item-writing commandments.

A   I   1.   Directions regarding how students should respond to classroom assessments intended to be especially challenging can occasionally be somewhat opaque in order to increase the assessment's difficulty.

A   I   2.   All student responses to essay tests should be first scored analytically, then scored holistically.

A   I   3.   Short-answer items, especially for young children, should employ direct questions rather than incomplete statements.

A   I   4.   To best assess students' ability to respond to essay items, allow students to choose among optional items.

A   I   5.   For essay items, make decisions regarding the importance of the mechanics of students' writing prior to scoring.

A   I   6.   When using blanks for short-answer incomplete statements, make sure the blanks for all items are equal in length.

A   I   7.   Construct all essay items so that a student's task is explicitly described.

A   I   8.   When teachers score their students' responses to essay questions, teachers should score all of a student's responses to different questions, then move on to the next student's responses.

A   I   9.   In order to help a teacher's more able students respond to essay questions, it is acceptable to employ fairly advanced vocabulary terms in the directions regarding how to respond to such questions.

A   I   10.   For short-answer items, place blanks for incomplete statements near the beginning of the statement.

A   I   11.   Provide students with the approximate time to be expended on each essay item as well as each item's value.

A   I   12.   For short-answer items employing incomplete statements, use at least two blanks per item, preferably more.

A   I   13.   Insofar as possible, classroom teachers should evaluate their students' essay responses anonymously, that is, without knowing which student wrote which response.

A   I   14.   Teachers should prepare a tentative scoring key after first scoring, say, a half-dozen students' responses to an essay item.

A   I   15.   Because part of the function of an essay item is to distinguish between high-achievers and low-achievers, it is not necessary for the items to be constructed so the student's task is described, in a way so that *all* students can understand the task.

CHAPTER 8

PERFORMANCE ASSESSMENT

Instructor to Instructor

Cautious Acceptance

Perhaps I have overreacted in this chapter to a phenomenon that I've witnessed more than a few times in the assessment behavior of classroom teachers. I refer to the assessment allure of performance testing and the likelihood that teachers, once hooked on it, tend to overuse it. As a consequence, many teachers burn out altogether on the utility of this excellent assessment strategy.

I'll bet I've known more than a dozen teachers who plunged into performance testing with gusto, only to limp away after a couple of years mumbling such things as "Never again!" or "Rubrics are rancid!" So, because I regard performance assessment as a powerful measurement procedure, I try to promote prudence in teachers' acceptance of it. I think performance assessment is wonderful. But to do it *well* takes far more time than most folks recognize. I'd rather see teachers properly use performance testing to measure a half-dozen or so powerful skills than see teachers do a shabby job with performance tests trying to assess a hoard of middle-level or lower-level skills. Some teachers I know, who several years ago were zealous proponents of performance testing, have now retreated to the assessment tranquility that comes with using only traditional, selected-response tests. That's a shame.

You can decide how much caution, if any, you want to toss out to your own students regarding the seductive appeal of performance testing.

Instructional Payoffs

When your students get to Chapter 12, and its attention to the *instructional dividends* of properly devised classroom assessments, I hope you can return for a brief re-look at Chapter 8's treatment of performance testing, especially in relation to the nature of the rubrics that are employed to evaluate students' responses to a performance test's task. As Chapter 12 attempts to make clear, the creation of an instructionally illuminating rubric can have a profoundly positive effect both on how a teacher teaches as well as how a learner learns.

Credible Evidence Needed

In Chapter 15, I will argue that a teacher's instructional quality should never be judged by students' scores on standardized achievement tests. Such tests are simply inappropriate for use in evaluating a teacher's (or a school staff's) instructional effectiveness.

But the public has a right to see if teachers are doing a good job. And the use of performance tests, because they ought to be employed to measure students' mastery of truly significant skills, can play a major role in producing such evidence.

In Chapter 13, your students will learn about a "split-and-switch" data-gathering design that they can employ to produce credible evidence of a teacher's instructional effectiveness. That data-gathering design, because it requires double assessment tasks, some student-juggling and, ideally, blind-scoring of students' responses by nonpartisan judges, should only be used for the assessment of really demanding cognitive skills. And those assessments should almost always consist of performance tests. Accordingly, after you reach Chapter 15, you might want to dip once more into Chapter 8's treatment of performance assessment.

A Real Problem

It's so easy to get caught up with the virtues of performance assessment that the problem of students' generalizable mastery will be overlooked. I encourage you to alert your students to that very genuine shortcoming of performance assessment. Even given the limited generalizability of performance testing, I still think it's a superb assessment approach for classroom teachers. But they need to recognize its limitations.

Activities

There are two potential activities set out for this chapter. First, you might ask your students to generate the top three evaluative criteria for judging students' responses to the performance-test task set forth in Figure 8.3. This activity forces students to prioritize the importance of the factors they would use to judge a student's performance. The second activity is a take-home-then-share endeavor. Students are given a week to create a performance test and rubric for a skill *similar in cognitive demand* to the one addressed in Figures 8.4 and 8.5. Then they bring their work to have it critiqued by another student and, if you wish, turned in for a grade. I've used this activity several times. It requires so much work from students that I've almost always made it a significant contributor to my students' grades. The trouble with that, of course, is that I have to read the blasted things!

Chapter Test

Performance tests are such substantial undertakings that it's difficult to come up with a terrific, yet terse, chapter test. What I've done here is lay out a fictional vignette of a teacher who engages in classroom-level performance testing, then asks for students to identify any serious errors the teacher has made. I don't think it's a terribly taxing test, because to make sure the teacher's errors are sufficiently discernible to be spotted, one needs to make them, not surprisingly, sufficiently discernible. I'm not sure that I'd use this chapter test if I were teaching a regular course about classroom assessment. As always, whether you do is up to you.

Answer Key. There are four fairly blatant mistakes that Mr. Caldwell made in carrying out performance assessment in his class. First, he did *too much of it*, making almost certain he'll not long continue to employ this assessment approach. Second, he used *too many evaluative criteria*. Third, he *never described levels of quality* from students' responses, only assigning mystery numbers based on *A*-through-*F* grades. Finally, he *applied both holistic and analytic scoring* to every response—an injudicious use of his time. Mr. Caldwell, as is often true with the recently converted, is way too zealous about performance testing.

Chapter Activities

♦♦♦ Ranking without Rankling

Ask your students to organize themselves into small groups, then carefully review the oral communications performance test described in the chapter's Figure 8.3. Having done so, each subgroup is to come up with the *three* (and only three) most significant evaluative criteria that would form the essence of a rubric that could be employed to evaluate the quality of students' responses to such a performance test. In order to render the rubric applicable to various kinds of one-on-one oral communications, each group should isolate evaluative criteria that would be suitable for judging students' responses to *any* of the types of tasks described in Figure 8.3.

You might suggest to the groups that they could first "brainstorm" potential evaluative criteria, then appraise and, ultimately, rank-order the criteria under consideration. When the group's analysis is over, however, only the top three evaluative criteria should be identified.

At this point in the activity, a certain amount of subgroup reporting to the entire class often proves illuminating.

♦♦♦ Build Your Own Performance Test

Direct your students to study the performance test described in Figure 8.4 and the associated rubric for evaluating students' responses seen in Figure 8.5. Ask students to use these figures as models, but to generate their own performance test and a rubric for scoring students' responses. Their performance tests should be aimed at measuring a cognitive skill similar in its challenge to the history skill set forth in the two figures.

After a week (or two), your students are to return their performance tests and exchange their tests, for peer critiquing purposes, with one other student for an in-class paired analysis of each other's efforts. After this peer critiquing, and some total-group discussion if you wish, you may choose to collect and grade each student's materials.

CHAPTER 8 TEST

Directions: Please read the following fictional vignette describing Mr. Caldwell's use of performance assessment in his classroom. Based on the material contained in Chapter 8, there is at least one mistake that the teacher made and, possibly, as many as five mistakes. In the response space provided, please briefly identify any rather blatant mistake(s) the teacher made in employing classroom-level performance assessment.

Mr. Caldwell teaches social studies classes in an inner-city high school. As part of a masters degree program that he is completing at a nearby university, Mr. Caldwell took a course last year in classroom assessment (and earned an *A*). This year, he is attempting to incorporate some of the things he learned in that class. In particular, he is trying to apply to his geography course what he has learned about performance testing.

Because the district's content standards for tenth-grade geography focus on 18 fairly specific skills, Mr. Caldwell uses a performance testing approach to measure students' mastery of each of those 18 geographic skills. Therefore, he tries to use a new performance test almost every week during the single semester that he teaches the geography course. Typically, students take a performance test on the last day of the week, and receive their graded responses back from Mr. Caldwell on the following Monday.

Mr. Caldwell believes that students' self-evaluation of their own geographic skills is crucial to their achievement. For each performance test, therefore, he develops a detailed rubric for them (and him) to use in judging their performances. He distributes this rubric to students at the beginning of instruction regarding each of the 18 skills. For each of the 18 skills, Mr. Caldwell has identified a minimum of 10 and a maximum of 15 evaluative criteria which, largely because of fairly clear labels, students seem to understand fairly well. For example, in a performance test dealing with Map Usage, one of the evaluative criteria is "Suitable Map-Type Chosen."

Then, for each of these labeled evaluative criteria, Mr. Caldwell assigns one-to-five points for each student's response. More points are better than fewer points. Mr. Caldwell indicates that the point allocations should roughly match an *A*-through-*F* grading system.

Although his weekends are busy, Mr. Caldwell grades each student's responses to that week's performance test using, first, a holistic scoring approach and, thereafter, an analytic scoring approach.

Although he is often exhausted by his implementation of performance assessment, Mr. Caldwell is convinced that the instructional dividends his students derive from this measurement approach make it well worthwhile. (And, of course, he wants to show that the *A* he earned in his classroom assessment course has paid off!)

****

What blatant mistake(s) did Mr. Caldwell make in his utilization of performance assessment?

_____

_____

_____

_____

_____

_____

_____

_____

_____

_____

_____

_____

_____

_____

CHAPTER 9

PORTFOLIO ASSESSMENT

Instructor to Instructor

Friends and Foes, Usually Fierce

Portfolio assessment has its strong proponents and its strong detractors. This appears to be one of those commodities that does not permit luke-warm responses. I've encountered teachers who organize their entire instructional programs around students' portfolios, teachers who truly believe that portfolio assessment is the most *instructionally beneficial* form of educational assessment. Yet, I've also run into just as many teachers who have given portfolio assessment a solid whirl, then come away dizzy. These "fallen away" portfoliophyles typically have abandoned portfolios simply because this form of educational measurement, although instructionally useful, is "too much blinking work."

I try very hard to avoid taking sides regarding this issue when I'm informing teachers or prospective teachers about portfolio assessment. I believe that certain types of individuals, largely because of their psychological makeup, can thrive in portfolio-land while others will surely flounder. Clearly, the kinds of content being taught also play a pivotal role in whether portfolios ought to be selected by a teacher as an assessment tool. But I encourage you to get your students to *think seriously* about the appropriateness or inappropriateness of portfolio assessment for their instructional situations.

When portfolio assessment works well, it is a wonder to behold. But, unfortunately, I see a good many teachers who have become almost intellectually eviscerated by the relentless time demands of portfolio assessment. As you'll note in the IRM, one of the suggested activities for this chapter calls for students to focus on the pros and cons of portfolio assessment. I've used this activity myself and found it helpful.

I find myself wondering, if portfolio assessment is so great, why don't I use it in my own graduate classes, especially classes in which students develop products to display their skill-mastery. And yet, except for one half-hearted effort to have students retain the classroom tests they had developed, I've never seriously used portfolio assessment in my own graduate classes. Am I being stupid or merely stubborn?

Activities

Two activities are suggested as possibilities for your consideration. First, there's a small-group debate regarding the wisdom of a teacher's embarking on a serious use of portfolio assessment. Second, a pair-based or group-based activity focuses on your students' understanding the fundamentals of portfolio assessment well enough to explain to someone else "how to do it."

Chapter Test

The test for this chapter deals exclusively with the seven "key ingredients" that were set out in the chapter. Students are given 10 statements based on those seven ingredients, the student's task being to decide which ones are true and which ones are false.

Answer Key. 1: F, 2: F, 3: T, 4: T, 5: T, 6: F, 7: T, 8: T, 9: F, 10: F.

Chapter Activities

♦♦♦ Portfolio Assessment's Pros and Cons

Split your class into subgroups, then alternately assign (at random) each subgroup to be Pro or Con regarding the merits of portfolio assessment. Be sure to end up with a similar number of Pro and Con groups. Ask each subgroup to think through a 5-10 minute argument that it could present to a group of *parents* regarding the virtues of portfolio assessment. Let the class know that one Pro Group and one Con Group will be selected at random to make a presentation to the rest of the class which will, at that point, assume the role of parents attending a back-to-school night.

Give the subgroups about 15 minutes to prepare their arguments. Then use a random-selection procedure to select the two groups who, in turn, present their arguments, pro and con, regarding the question: "Should portfolio assessment be used more widely in this school?"

At the close of the presentations, allow "parents" to ask any questions they wish to raise or to make any comments they wish. After this question and comment period, you may want to discuss the most cogent arguments presented by both groups.

♦♦♦ How To Do It

In pairs or small groups, ask students to prepare a brief description of what portfolio assessment is and how to implement a portfolio assessment program. Each pair or small group should prepare a description that would be suitable for presentation to the faculty of a middle school that was exploring the suitability of portfolio assessment for their own classes. The presentations should be complete enough to allow a teacher to register a positive or a negative reaction to what, at this point in the activity, they understand "portfolio assessment" to be.

Then select one or two groups (pairs) to make their presentation to the rest of your class which, for this activity, assumes the role of a middle school faculty. After the presentation(s), discuss whether any important elements in portfolio assessment were omitted or misrepresented in the oral presentations.

CHAPTER 9 TEST

Directions: The following statements are based on the "key ingredients" of portfolio assessment presented in the chapter. Read each statement, then indicate whether it is true or false by circling the appropriate letter.

T or F   1.   Because students' parents can ordinarily become heavily involved in portfolio assessment, a teacher's first task is to make sure that parents "own" their child's portfolio.

T or F   2.   Fortunately, well organized teachers do not need to devote much time to the conduct of portfolio conferences.

T or F   3.   When held, portfolio conferences should not only deal with the evaluation of a student's work products, but should also improve the student's self-evaluation abilities.

T or F   4.   In general, a wide variety of work products should be included in a portfolio rather than a limited range of work products.

T or F   5.   In order for students to evaluate their own efforts, the evaluative criteria to be used in judging a portfolio's work products must be identified, then made known to students.

T or F   6.   Students should rarely be involved in the determination of the evaluative criteria by which a portfolio's products will be appraised.

T or F   7.   Early in a school year, a teacher who is using a portfolio assessment should make sure the students' parents understand the portfolio process.

T or F   8.   Parents should become actively involved in reviewing the work products in a child's portfolio.

T or F   9.   Students should be asked to review their own work products only at a time near the end of the school year so that their self-evaluations can be more accurate.

T or F   10.   Students' work products must be stored in file folders, then placed in a lockable metal file cabinet to prevent unauthorized use of a student's portfolio.

CHAPTER 10

AFFECTIVE ASSESSMENT

Instructor to Instructor

Motivation Considerations

As you can probably infer from what I've written in this chapter, I think students' affect is truly important. Nevertheless, I rarely see teachers routinely incorporating any affective assessment instruments in their classroom measurement devices. Cognitive tests, or so it seems, simply drive out any sort of affective assessments.

Your own position regarding the importance of affect will surely influence how you tackle this chapter. If you share my views, you'll try to encourage your students to get serious about assessing their students' affect. And to do so, of course, will require that they learn how to measure key affective variables. In my own classes, I try to devote equal time to the "how-to" and to the "why" of affective assessment. If my students master the "how-to," but aren't convinced of the "why-do-it," then there's little likelihood they'll use the assessment procedures they've mastered.

If, however, you do not subscribe to my views regarding affect's import, then you'll approach this chapter quite differently. A number of colleagues whom I sincerely respect do not believe that affective assessment is as significant as I do. You may share their sentiments. If so, of course, you'll surely bang harder on the "how-to" drum than the "why-do-it" drum.

A Long Overdue Revision

One of the most useful books I've relied on over the years was one written about affective assessment by Lorin Anderson. Originally published in 1981, Lorin and Sid Bourke brought out a second edition in 2000. That's about a two-decade delay! I've suggested to Lorin that the field's "insatiable demand" for a revision must have been fairly modest!

Fortunately, the reworked and improved book is every bit as useful as its antique predecessor. I encourage you to get a copy. It's cited at the chapter's close. I hope Lorin and Sid remain in good health. They probably are already working on a third edition slated for release in 2020 A.D.!

New Inventories

One of the suggestions I received from several of the publisher-hired external reviewers who looked over the second edition of *Classroom Assessment* was that I needed to include more illustrative Likert affective inventories. I did so in the third edition, chiefly as an appendix for this chapter. They're also present in the fourth edition, once more as an appendix. Those inventories, all of which I've personally tried out with small groups of students, are written at about the right level of detail (I believe) for use by classroom teachers. If you don't agree, feel free to massage them into better shape. I've never created an assessment device in my life that couldn't be improved by collegial critiquing.

In particular, you may need to call your students' attention to the use of only one or two items to deal with a particular affective variable. Unlike the chapter's eight-step description of how to churn out a bona fide Likert inventory, the appendicized inventories illustrate what a typical teacher's real-world affective inventories are apt to be like.

Activities

A great project that I've often used myself is to have my students develop a full-blown Likert inventory following all eight steps in the chapter's directives about how to build such an inventory. This is typically a two-week, take-home assignment. Activity one describes how you might carry out such an assignment. The second activity asks your students to debate the importance of affective assessment in a typical teacher's classroom. Finally, the third chapter activity asks your students to identify the five most important affective variables they think a teacher should assess—assuming the teacher intends to assess students' affect.

Chapter Test

The chapter test combines a binary-choice format (correct-incorrect) with short-answer items. The students who spot an incorrect procedure being carried out by the teacher must then indicate how the teacher should correct that procedural error. Typically, I give students two points for a properly identified correct procedure, two points for a properly identified *and corrected* incorrect procedure, and one point for a properly identified but poorly repaired incorrect procedure. This kind of scoring scheme, I readily admit, was not created on some sort of Psychometric Olympus. If you used the chapter test, score it any darn way you like!

Answer Key. 1: IN (Remedy: Select noncontroversial affective targets for assessment.), 2: IN (Remedy: Do not ask for handwritten, hence potentially identifiable, student suggestions or, if important, ask students to submit such suggestions on sheets separate from the Likert inventories.), 3: C, 4: IN (Remedy: She should use a pre-instruction as well as a post-instruction assessment to account for differences in her students' *entry* attitudes.), 5: C, 6: C, 7: C, 8: IN (Remedy: Mrs. Hashizuma should have made her announcement about the collection method *before* students began to complete their inventories. The idea with such anonymity-enhancement collection methods is to induce honest responding by students. A post-completion announcement would have had no positive impact on the candor of students' responses.), 9: C, 10: IN (Remedy: Ms. Stafford's confidence notwithstanding, students' anonymity must be preserved if they are apt to respond truthfully. Otherwise, students are likely to produce "socially desirable" responses instead of honest ones. Inferences about individual students, therefore, are likely to be invalid. Ms. Stafford should employ anonymously completed inventories and be satisfied with valid *group-based* inferences.)

<h1 style="text-align:center">Chapter Activities</h1>

♦♦♦ Build Your Own, Bob!

For the first activity, one that typically takes two or three weeks to complete, ask students to build a 10-item Likert affective inventory for a single affective variable such as students' self-esteem as learners. In other words, rather than creating an affective inventory such as those presented in the chapter appendix in which an affective dimension is often assessed with only two items, your students are to construct an inventory dealing with a single, more encompassing affective dimension, that is, the kind of affective dimension that 10 or more different kinds of statements could be employed in concert to assess.

Ask your students to carry out all eight steps of the chapter-recommended procedure for creating a Likert inventory. Then, ask your students to prepare brief (two-page or three-page maximum) descriptions of the process and an appraisal of the resultant inventory. The final form of the inventory should, of course, also be turned in. During the class session when these inventories and reports are to be submitted, a useful discussion of 30 or more minutes can usually be held focusing on "Lessons Learned from Doing Affective Assessment."

♦♦♦ To Assess or Not To Assess: Is That a Question?

Split your students into small groups, then alternately assign either pro or con groups regarding the following question: "Affective assessment should have little, if any, role in a typical teacher's classroom assessment program."

After allowing the groups to caucus and plan for about 15-20 minutes, then select at random a pro and a con group to take turns giving their arguments on their designated side of the issue. At the close of the oral presentations, an open class discussion of the most potent pro and con arguments often proves illuminating.

♦♦♦ Rank Those Outcomes!

This activity presumes that a teacher has decided to assess students' affect, first, at the outset and, later, at the close of a school year. Assuming that a teacher intends to use 10-item self-report inventories similar to those found in the chapter appendix, with two items per affective variable (one item stated positively and one stated negatively), the task is to decide on the five, *and only five*, affective variables to assess.

Split your class into subgroups, then ask each group to identify a specific type of teacher, that is, a grade-level elementary teacher or a subject area secondary teacher. Then, using brainstorming followed by ranking procedures, each group should come up with the five affective outcomes to be assessed.

Ask several groups to describe their final set of affective assessment targets. See if there are any similarities in the affective variables chosen, especially for subgroups pursuing comparable grade levels or subject matters.

CHAPTER 10 TEST

Directions: Presented below are fictional vignettes describing procedures being carried out by teachers who wish to engage in affective assessment of their students. Read each vignette, then indicate whether the described procedure was *Correct* (Circle the C.) or *Incorrect* (Circle the IN.). For any item that you indicated described an incorrect procedure, you should then *briefly describe* how the teacher should rectify the teacher's error. Use the spaces provided to suggest a way to remedy the fictional teacher's error.

1. Mr. Evans uses an anonymous self-report affective inventory to gauge students' current preferences regarding highly visible Republican and Democratic political figures. (C or IN?)

    If IN, then how to remedy? _____

    _____

    _____.

2. Mrs. Peterson collects monthly affective inventories (entitled *How am I Doing?*) from the students in her instructional technology classes. She not only uses anonymous Likert-type inventories, but also encourages students to suggest ways that she could improve her teaching. (C or IN?)

    If IN, then how to remedy? _____

    _____

    _____

3. Ms. Johnson asks her fourth-grade students, on a pretest and posttest basis, to complete anonymously a self-report Likert inventory about their interest in the subjects she teaches. Ms. Johnson uses students' responses to arrive at a group-based inference about the aggregate interests of her students. (C or IN?)

    If IN, then how to remedy? _____

    _____

    _____.

4. Miss Meadows assesses her English students' affect at the end of each semester. She then arrives at interpretations regarding the attitudes toward English of each class of students. (C or IN?)

    If IN, then how to remedy? _____

    _____

    _____

5. When creating a Likert affective inventory for his French classes, Mr. Bouvier asks a group of his colleagues to review draft statements for his new inventory. Any statements that his colleagues do not *universally* classify as positive or negative are discarded by Mr. Bouvier. (C or IN?)

    If IN, then how to remedy? _____

    _____

    _____.

6. When Ms. Marks tries out an early version of a Likert inventory intended to assess students' interest in pursuing a post-secondary education, she discovers that three of her statements do not function in the same way as the draft inventory's other statements. Accordingly, she discards the three atypically functioning statements. (C or IN?)

    If IN, then how to remedy? _____

    _____

    _____.

7. Mrs. Chappel teaches third-grade students. In an effort to form an inference about her students' attitudes toward mathematics, she uses a five-item Likert inventory with only three response options (that is, Agree, Not Sure, Disagree) rather than the five levels of disagreement often used for older children (that is, Strongly Agree, Agree, Uncertain, Disagree, Strongly Disagree). (C or IN?)

    If IN, then how to remedy? _____

    _____

    _____.

8. Mrs. Hashizuma has her students complete self-report affective inventories at the beginning of each school year. Then, just as the inventories have been completed, she announces that students are to go to the back of the room and place their completed inventories in a large box intended for that purpose. (C or IN?)

If IN, then how to remedy? _____

_____

_____.

9. Mr. Gomez is confident that the parents of his sixth-grade students will uniformly want their children to possess positive attitudes toward learning. Accordingly, he develops a 10-item self-report inventory dealing with such attitudes. He administers it anonymously at the beginning and end of each school year. (C or IN?)

If IN, then how to remedy? _____

_____

_____.

10. Ms. Stafford is convinced that she can make accurate inferences about the affective status of individual students, and thereupon can make better instructional decisions about them. Accordingly, she asks students to write their names on the reverse side of their attitude inventories. (C or IN?)

If IN, then how to remedy? _____

_____

_____.

CHAPTER 11

IMPROVING TEACHER-DEVELOPED ASSESSMENTS

Instructor to Instructor

An Appropriate Level of Interest

Most experienced teachers or teachers-in-training don't get all that excited about this chapter's contents. I can understand why. In particular, the empirical item-improvement procedures are often seen as too off-puttingly quantitative and, beyond that, as way too much trouble for an already busy teacher.

Personally, I tend to get more charged up by this chapter than the folks I'm teaching. I especially enjoy its data-based item-improvement procedures. They are so deliciously numerical and, in addition, there are rather clear guidelines about the good and bad features of particular test items.

You'll have to decide how much you encourage your students to comprehend this chapter's contents. Recognizing my own proclivities, I usually try to overcompensate a bit by urging the systematic use of judgmental item-improvement approaches. What I most fear is that teachers will whomp up a test, then *never* devote any time to making that test better. I try to generate just enough interest in the chapter so my students *know* how to improve their tests empirically but actually *might* improve their tests judgmentally.

Demystification

One reason I try to get my own students familiar with empirical item-improvement techniques is that the procedures described in the chapter are fundamentally the same as those used by commercial testing companies as they create and improve their achievement and aptitude tests.

The better idea that a teacher has about the way such improvement-activities are carried out, the more likely it is the teacher will be able to understand the appropriate/inappropriate uses of commercially published standardized tests. The item-improvement procedures employed by commercial testing houses are surely more sophisticated than the techniques described in this chapter. But, at bottom, they are doing the same job in essentially the same way. Teachers need to know this. The less intimidated that teachers are by commercially created high-stakes tests, the better it will be for students.

Activities

Three possible activities are provided for this chapter. The first asks students to develop group-presentations contrasting judgmental and empirical item-improvement procedures. The second, focused on empirical item-improvement approaches, asks groups of students to create a set of fictitious data suggesting the need for possible item improvements. Finally, the third activity asks pairs of students to devise a practical time-sensible approach to item improvement for a typical real-world classroom teacher.

Chapter Test

This 10-item chapter test contains binary-choice items asking whether fictional teachers made the *right decision* or *wrong decision* with respect to item revision.

Chapter Activities

♦♦♦ Judgmental or Empirical?

Ask your students to split into small groups and plan brief oral presentations describing the differences between judgmental and empirical item improvement techniques. Ask them to prepare their presentations as though they would be giving those presentations to a group of first-year teachers.

Then, after sufficient planning time, randomly select one or two groups who should present to the remainder of the class. At that time, the "audience" members should assume the role of first year teachers.

After the presentations, a general class discussion of the two item-improvement strategies should help your students understand more clearly what the fundamental differences are between the two approaches.

♦♦♦ Show Me The Data!

Split your class into small groups, then ask each group to create a minimum of three (or any minimum you prefer) sets of fictitious data reflecting on the quality of an item. The item itself need not be created, only the fictitious empirical results of using the item with a class of students. Examples of suitable kinds of p values, discrimination indices, or distractor analyses will be found in the chapter. In essence, this activity asks the subgroups to come up with new sets of fictitious data indicating whether an item should or should not be improved. For each set of data, the group should itself decide whether the data warrant either an "Improve" or "Don't Improve" decision.

Then, after ample preparation time, ask all groups to exchange their sets of empirical data with another to see if the new subgroup's decision coincides with that of the originating group. The originating group's decisions should be kept secret until the second group has arrived at its own decisions about the items.

♦♦♦ What's Reasonable?

Organize your class into two-person teams, each of which is to prepare a presentation suitable for a group of experienced teachers. The topic of the presentation is the following: "What is a reasonable approach to improving teacher-developed assessments in the real world?"

After providing sufficient preparation time, randomly choose several of the groups to make their presentations orally to the rest of the students who, at that moment, is supposed to react like a group of seasoned classroom teachers whose "quest for sanity" should guide their reactions to any pair's presentation.

CHAPTER 11 TEST

Directions: Please read each of the following descriptions of classroom teachers who are deciding whether to revise items from their classroom tests. For each description, indicate whether the described teacher made the *Right decision* (Circle the R.) or the *Wrong decision* (Circle the W.).

R or W   1.   Mr. Hubbart, a science teacher, reviews the content of his own tests that he created two years ago. He discovers that the content in a half-dozen items has been rendered inaccurate by recent studies published in scientific research journals. Without checking with any colleagues, he decides to revise the half-dozen items so that they are consistent with the latest research findings. Was Mr. Hubbart's decision *right* or *wrong*?

R or W   2.   Mrs. Chang, a fifth-grade teacher, asks a colleague to review her major examinations. The colleague has recently completed a graduate course in classroom assessment and has expressed a willingness to help other teams improve their classroom tests. The colleague identifies about 10 items that clearly violate item-writing rules based on the item-type involved. Mrs. Chang decides to change the items as suggested because in all 10 items, as she re-examines them, do appear to have problems. Was Mrs. Chang's decision *right* or *wrong*?

R or W   3.   A sixth-grade teacher, Mrs. Jones, has subjected her major tests (which she hopes will yield accurate criterion-referenced inferences) to a pretest-posttest type of item analysis. Because she discovers that almost all of her items reflect substantial pre-to-post increases in the number of students' correct responses, Mrs. Jones decides to make about half of her items more difficult so that students' pre-to-post improvements will not be so pronounced. Was Mrs. Jones' decision *right* or *wrong*?

R or W   4.   Mr. Villa uses one of his chemistry tests to discriminate among students so the most able students can take part in a special competition sponsored by the National Science Foundation. A testing specialist at the school district's office has performed several analyses on Mr. Villa's items that indicate at least a fourth of the items on this test have discrimination indices of less than .15. Seeing these results, Mr. Villa decides to alter those items so that they might discriminate more efficiently. Was Mr. Villa's decision *right* or *wrong*?

R or W   5.   Miss Jenkins subjects her end-of-unit exams, all of which contain four-option multiple-choice items, to extensive analyses after she has administered them. Presented below is a distractor analysis for one of her final exam's items in a unit that, based on other posttest results, seems to be a well-taught unit:

Item No. 18	Answer Options				
$p = .33$ $D = 0.0$	A	B	C*	D	Omit
Upper Half-Class	7	0	5	1	2
Lower Half-Class	1	1	5	4	4

* Correct Response

Because of the p value and discrimination index for this item, Miss Jenkins decides to leave the item as is. Was Miss Jenkins' decision *right* or *wrong*?

R or W   6.   Mr. Robinson decides to eliminate all items from his pretest on which students score too well. He plans to eliminate most subsequent instruction dealing with the content represented by those items. He finds that four of his pretest's items have p values of .20 or less. As a result, he decides to replace each of these easy items with more difficult ones. Was Mr. Robinson's decision *right* or *wrong*?

R or W   7.   Mr. Gurtiza teaches English to high school seniors. Although he employs writing samples to assess students' composition skills, many items in his tests are selected-response in nature. To improve his exams, Mr. Gurtiza asks his students, as they are taking their exams, to circle the numbers of any multiple-choice items that they find need revisions because of ambiguity, incorrectness, and so on. Mr. Gurtiza then tallies the frequency of items whose numbers have been circled. He decides to discard or modify any item circled by at least 20 percent of his students. Was Mr. Gurtiza's decision *right* or *wrong*?

R or W   8.   Mr. Goldberg, a kindergarten teacher, has recently compared his observation-based classroom assessments with the recently state-approved *Content Standards for Kindergartners*. He discovered that fully five of the new content standards are not even addressed in his observation-based assessments. Accordingly, he decides to alter his observation instrument so that all of the new state-sanctioned kindergarten content standards will be represented by his classroom tests. Was Mr. Goldberg's decision *right* or *wrong*?

R or W   9. Although Ms. Thompson wants her classroom tests to provide evidence for her to make criterion-referenced interpretations about each of her students' current achievement levels, she still wants her tests to be "technically superior." As a consequence, she has decided to replace all of the binary-choice items in her test for which students' response data indicate the items are negative discriminators or nondiscriminators. Was Ms. Thompson's decision *right* or *wrong*?

R or W   10. Mr. Acura has persuaded a colleague to administer Mr. Acura's seventh-grade science test to the colleague's seventh-grade social studies students (who have not yet taken a science class). Mr. Acura, who wants his classroom assessments to yield criterion-referenced interpretations about his students, is delighted to learn that in the item-by-item comparisons between the "instructed" science students and the "uninstructed" social studies students, Mr. Acura's science students dramatically out-perform their social studies counterparts. Mr. Acura decides to leave his tests largely unaltered. Was Mr. Acura's decision *right* or *wrong*?

CHAPTER 12

INSTRUCTIONALLY ORIENTED ASSESSMENT

Instructor to Instructor

A New Notion

Whenever I teach a classroom assessment course, most of my students are genuinely surprised by the idea that tests can help teachers *teach*. Indeed, this notion is frequently so foreign to the way they've always thought about tests that I often have to engage in some flat-out coaxing to get them to view the assessment-instruction linkage a bit differently.

Clearly, experienced teachers typically possess years of traditional thinking about the most appropriate moment a test should be born. And that tradition says tests are created *after* instruction is over, or at least pretty well over. Such a traditional view of classroom testing, of course, stems largely from the idea that the chief mission of classroom tests is to help teachers dish out grades to students.

Well, this chapter extols a different way of thinking about classroom assessment. The chapter suggests that properly constructed classroom tests can be a boon to a teacher's instructional decision-making. In this chapter I've tried to persuade readers they need to "break set," that is, they need to think about classroom testing in an altogether different way. They need to think about testing as a key that can unlock far more effective approaches to teaching. Most of my students need to be persuaded that I'm not shucking them. This chapter, therefore, often takes me a couple of weeks to cover. There's the content, of course; and then there's the coaxing!

Rampant Rubricity

I've found that one of the best ways to illustrate the *instructional* payoffs of well-formed tests is to show my students how it is that different sorts of rubrics can or cannot contribute to a teacher's instructional decision-making. Whereas hypergeneral and task-specific rubrics have almost no instructional-planning dividends, a skill-focused rubric supplies all sorts of guidance regarding (1) how a teacher should deliver instruction and (2) how students can inform themselves if they are moving toward skill-mastery.

A good many of my students are only familiar with the kinds of rubrics that have historically been used to evaluate students' writing samples. And, my students often assume, because such rubrics seem to have been instructionally useful, maybe it's true that all rubrics can be helpful to a teacher. But although almost all the *writing*-sample rubrics I've ever seen are skill-focused in nature, *most* of the rubrics I've seen that are to be used with other skills are not. More often than I've hoped, rubrics devised to judge students' mastery of cognitive skills in other subjects typically turn out to be hypergeneral or task-specific in nature. And those sorts of rubrics, as the chapter suggests, are next to worthless for instructional planning purposes.

So, if you can get your students to see that certain sorts of rubrics help teachers make solid instructional decisions while other kinds of rubrics don't, then perhaps you can make the same point about classroom tests themselves. For it is true that a selected-response or a constructed-response classroom test can, if created with instructional decision-making foremost in the test-creator's mind, help teachers make more appropriate decisions about their teaching.

This "new" way of thinking about classroom tests will, in my experience, require some serious support and continuing advocacy from the person who introduces the notion. Good luck.

Activities

Three potential activities are described for this chapter. First, subgroups of students are called on to devise oral presentations to convince prospective teachers that they should regard classroom tests as vehicles to help teachers do a more effective instructional job. Second, students are asked to prepare two or three actual rubrics, at least one of which is a skill-focused rubric. Finally, students are asked, in pairs or subgroups, to identify potentially successful persuasion schemes that could be employed to convince "traditionalist" teachers that there is merit in their use of instructionally oriented assessments.

Chapter Test

The test for this chapter consists of ten multiple-choice items, each focused on an important aspect of the chapter's content.

Answer Key. 1: C, 2: A, 3: C, 4: D, 5: B, 6: A, 7: A, 8: B, 9: D, 10: B.

Chapter Activities

♦♦♦ Can Tests Really Help Teaching?

Divide your class into subgroups, then ask each subgroup to prepare a brief *persuasive* oral presentation that could be given to a group of teacher education students who were in the final stages of their preparation to be teachers. The presentation should stress the instructional dividends derivative from instructionally illuminating classroom tests. In essence, each group's presentation should focus on the need for these prospective teachers to "think differently" about classroom tests. Each group should prepare a compelling, hopefully motivating presentation that would incline these teachers-in-training to use instructionally oriented tests when they begin their teaching careers.

Then choose one or more groups to make their oral presentations to the rest of your class who, at that point, you ask to assume the role of teachers-in-training. A post-presentation whole-group analysis of the presentation(s) will typically prove to be useful.

◆◆◆ Roll Out Your Rubrics

Ask each student to develop two or three rubrics during the interval between your class meetings. (I've often allowed a week for this development.) One of the rubrics must be a skill-focused rubric and the other(s) a hypergeneral and/or task-specific rubric. The type of rubric is *not* to be identified by the student. Require your students to make a half-dozen copies of each rubric developed.

Then, on the day the rubrics are to be turned in (You are to get one copy for grading purposes.), split your class in a subgroup of about five or six students, then distribute the rubrics for a group-review activity. Ask each group to read the same rubric at one time, deciding as a group *which kind* of rubric it appears to be, that is, skill-focused, hypergeneral, or task-specific. After all rubrics have been "identified," ask the rubrics' authors to indicate whether the subgroup's identification was accurate or not. Disagreements can be resolved by you or via full-class discussion.

◆◆◆ Pick Your Persuasion Ploys

In pairs or small groups, have your students attempt to isolate what they believe would represent the most powerful persuasion procedures to influence a seasoned teacher, a teacher who views tests exclusively from a "test-so-as-to-grade" perspective, to embrace instructionally oriented assessment. Then ask different pairs (or groups) to describe or demonstrate the persuasion ploys they have chosen.

CHAPTER 12 TEST

Directions: For each of the items below, please select the *best* answer.

---

1. What is the distinguishing feature of a *task-specific rubric*?

    A. It is applicable to a wide variety of tasks.
    B. It deals with atypically challenging cognitive skills.
    C. It applies to the scoring of students' responses to a single task.
    D. It is a guide used to assess a student's specific knowledge.

2. Which of the following instructional decision should be *least* influenced by results of classroom assessments?

    A. When to start teaching something
    B. What to teach
    C. How long to teach something
    D. How effective instruction was

3. Traditionally, what has been the *sequential* relationship among assessment, curriculum, and instruction?

    A. Generally, teachers considered instruction, then curriculum, then assessment.
    B. Generally, teachers considered assessment, then curriculum, then instruction.
    C. Generally, teachers considered curriculum, then instruction, then assessment.
    D. Generally, teachers considered curriculum, then assessment, then instruction.

4. Which of the following is *not* a typical planning dividend of instructionally illuminating assessments?

    A. More lucid explanations
    B. More on-target practice activities
    C. More accurate task analyses
    D. More valid score-based inferences

5. One *defensible* way of conserving instructional time rather than using classroom time for assessment purposes is to:

    A. assess only certain children
    B. employ item sampling
    C. test more frequently but with shorter tests
    D. rely exclusively on constructed-response items

6. What is the distinguishing feature of a *hypergeneral rubric*?

    A. Such a rubric contains only very general and imprecise evaluative criteria.
    B. Such a rubric is generally applicable to a wide range of students' responses.
    C. Such a rubric reflects remarkably clear rules for the appraisal of students' responses.
    D. Such a rubric offers general instructional guidance to those charged with teaching a skill.

7. Which of the following is *not* a rule that should be followed in constructing a *skill-focused rubric*?

    A. Employ at least a half-dozen well stated evaluative criteria.
    B. Be certain that the skill to be assessed is significant.
    C. Provide a concise label for each evaluative criterion.
    D. Match the length of the rubric to the rubric-user's tolerance for detail.

8. Which of the following is an important rule that should be followed when creating an instructionally illuminating test composed of selected-response items?

    A. All selected-response items must, at least conceptually, be able to be developed in the form of short-answer items.
    B. Prior to the test's creation, the complete domain of assessable knowledge must be identified.
    C. At least one-fourth of the knowledge actually assessed by the selected-response items must be essentially unanticipatable by students.
    D. Selected-response tests of students' factual knowledge, in order to be comprehensive, must assess the entire domain of assessed knowledge.

9.   What is a key advantage of an instructionally illuminating test that has been created prior to a teacher's instructional planning?

A.   It makes a teacher think about assessment choices even before thinking about instructional choices.
B.   Because it has been developed prior to a teacher's actual instruction, it will not be influenced adversely by ineffective instruction.
C.   An advance-developed test makes it more likely that a classroom teacher can inject suitable affectively oriented instruction into lessons.
D.   It exemplifies, and thus clarifies for teachers, the instructional outcomes to be sought for students.

10.   Well-constructed rubrics are most effectively employed, *from an instructional perspective*, with respect to:

A.   the generation of instructional sequences suitable for promoting important affective variables.
B.   planning instruction for the promotion of high-level cognitive skills assessed by constructed-response tests.
C.   the measurement of the lowest-level objectives based on Bloom's Cognitive Taxonomy.
D.   the assessment of students' cognitive skills as measured by varied selected-response tests.

CHAPTER 13

MAKING SENSE OUT OF STANDARDIZED TEST SCORES

Instructor to Instructor

A Nuts and Bolts Chapter

Many teachers have a rough notion of how to interpret students' scores on standardized achievement tests; but many teachers don't. I'd even guess that *most* teachers would be awash if asked to describe how best to make sense out of standardized test results. And it is this absence of knowledge that usually makes this chapter a fairly easy one to teach. Most teachers, or teachers-in-training, really would like to understand the most prominent ways of interpreting students' performances on standardized tests—not only those national tests distributed by commercial test publishers—but also those high-stakes tests developed specifically for states or districts.

If your students can leave this chapter with a reasonable idea about what makes a percentile purr or how not to stumble over a stanine, then that's the general level of understanding most teachers need. And, because most teachers realize that they need to know such stuff when dealing with parents, this chapter usually captures most of my students' attention.

These days, with scores on standardized tests featured so heavily in the news, I can't imagine being a teacher who would be easily flummoxed by parents' simple questions about the interpretation of standardized test scores. So all teachers, even those whose instructional effectiveness does not seem to hang on students' standardized test scores, definitely need to master the rudiments of test-score interpretation that are addressed in this chapter.

Two New Interpretation Indices

In the earlier editions of *Classroom Assessment*, I only treated three interpretation indices in this chapter, namely, percentiles, grade equivalents, and scale scores. I chose those three because they were the ones I continued to encounter when working with real-world educators in the schools.

But when the book's publisher sent the second edition to external reviewers in order to get some ideas about how to spiffy up the third edition, two of those five reviewers suggested I add stanines and normal curve equivalents to this chapter. Two out of five. That's 40 percent! Faced with such a reviewer landslide, I meekly complied. (Fortunately, the external reviewers for the fourth edition appeared to be satisfied with the added content.) I was reluctant to deflect readers from genuine familiarity with the original three, so I admittedly gave stanines and NCEs just a "lick and a promise." (I sometimes wonder what my parents meant when they used that expression.) If you feel the need to lather up a more intense treatment of the two new add-ons, please do so.

Activities

Two activities are suggested for this chapter's treatment. The first one involves the use of an actual score-reporting form intended for teachers or parents. This means that you'll need to be on the lookout for such a report form early during the course. If you don't have one, and are working with teachers, you should be able to ask them to locate such a form for you (if, of course, you plan to employ the initially suggested activity.).

The second activity is a fairly prosaic one. It asks pairs of students to work up brief, yet communicate descriptions of the five score-interpretation indices dealt with in the chapter. This second activity may not bristle with inventiveness, but I've often used it and, not surprisingly in view of what we've learned about the instructional payoff of "engaged time-on-task," the activity works!

Chapter Test

As a change of pace, and to illustrate an issue you might wish to address, the test for this chapter features multiple-choice items—but items containing only three alternatives. As a consequence, I suspect your students will surely find it easier than a test containing four-alternative items or five-alternative items. If you use the chapter test (And, to be honest, it's a pretty soft one.), you might want to have your class consider the virtues of different numbers of answer options for their own multiple-choice tests.

Answer Key. 1: C, 2: B, 3: B, 4: A, 5: B, 6: C, 7: A, 8: B, 9: A, 10: C.

Chapter Activities

♦♦♦ An Interpretational Puzzle

If you can gain access to a score-reporting form that is sent to a student's parents, or to a student's teacher, make sufficient copies for all your students. Then distribute the photocopied forms, split the class into subgroups, and ask each subgroup to create five-to-ten (your choice) True-False items based directly on the score-reporting form. Then, after the items are available, have groups exchange their items with another group so that the recipient group can, by consensus, arrive at a True or False response for each item. The recipient group then gives its answers to the item-writing group to see if all items have been answered "correctly." Disagreements can be discussed with the entire class.

Nutshell Descriptions

Ask your students to form pairs, then have each pair prepare a three-sentence written description (a total 100-word maximum) for *each* of the following test-score interpretation indicators: percentile, grade equivalents, scale scores, stanines, and normal curve equivalents. Having allowed sufficient preparation time, randomly call on different pairs so that two descriptions (in a row) of each indicator are given. Then pause to have a total-group discussion of the adequacy of the two descriptions.

CHAPTER 13 TEST

Directions: Choose the best answer for each of the following three-option, multiple-choice items.

1. Parents who want their children to score high on standardized achievement tests would be most happy if their child earned which of the following percentiles?

    A. 50th
    B. 2nd
    C. 99th

2. If two sets of test scores indicate that Score-Set X has a standard deviation of 10.2, while Score-Set Y, on the same test, has a standard deviation of 8.4, what does this mean?

    A. Students in the Score-Set X outperformed their Score-Set Y counterparts.
    B. The performances of the X students were more variable than those of the Y students.
    C. The scores of the Y students were more spread out than those of the X students.

3. Which of the following is *not* a group-focused index employed in the interpretation of students' test performances?

    A. Standard Deviation
    B. Raw score
    C. Median

4. Which of the following score-interpretation options is most *readily interpretable*?

    A. Percentiles
    B. NCEs
    C. Grade equivalents

5. Which of the following score-interpretation options is *most often misunderstood*?

    A. Stanines
    B. Grade equivalents
    C. Percentiles

6. Which of the following score-interpretation options is especially useful in equalizing the disparate difficulty levels of different test forms?

    A. Percentiles
    B. Grade equivalents
    C. Scale scores

7. *Most* score-interpretation indices rely on a fundamentally similar interpretational framework. That framework is best described as:

    A.   relative
    B.   absolute
    C.   arbitrary

8. If a student's raw score was at the 45th percentile, in what stanine would the student have scored?

    A.   Fourth
    B.   Fifth
    C.   Sixth

9. Which of the following score-interpretation indices were initially introduced to permit amalgamation of students' scores on different standardized tests?

    A.   Normal curve equivalents
    B.   Stanines
    C.   Grade equivalents

10. Which one of the following three ways of interpreting standardized test scores has a descriptive statistical function fundamentally different than the other two?

    A.   Range
    B.   Standard deviation
    C.   Mean

CHAPTER 14

APPROPRIATE AND INAPPROPRIATE TEST-PREPARATION PRACTICES

Instructor to Instructor

Significant Stuff

This chapter deals with an issue about which I have strong sentiments. I believe that today's pressures on teachers to improve test scores, fueled by NCLB, have led to educationally sordid test-preparation practices by way too many teachers. In a sense, these teachers are victims in a score-boosting game that they haven't a chance to win. (Chapter 15 will, hopefully, make that clear.) Yet, exonerating circumstances aside, what's going on in many of our nation's classrooms is harming children. Score-boosting is being practiced; true education is being abandoned. And all of this is taking place, in my view, because most of our teachers have not given any serious thought to the topic of how students *should* and *shouldn't* be prepared to perform on high-stakes tests.

I think that the vast majority of our nation's teachers want what's best for kids. And, if those teachers ever thought seriously about how their test-preparation practices are harming children, tawdry test-prep practices would be abandoned without delay. But most teachers haven't thought *at all* about what sorts of test-preparation are appropriate and what sorts of test-preparation aren't. After they leave this chapter, with your help, they ought to know better how to deal with test-preparation issues.

Two Commandments

About 10 years ago, when I began to encounter more and more frequent instances of teachers' inappropriate test preparation, I concluded that the two chief contributors to this unsuitable preparation were (1) the pressure to raise students' scores on high-stakes accountability tests and (2) the failure of teachers to have devoted any serious thinking to how an inappropriate instance of test preparation could be educationally damaging to children. I couldn't do much about diminishing the score-boosting pressures induced by high-stakes tests, but I thought I might be able to help a bit with the second contributor, namely, teachers' lack of conversance with issues linked to test preparation.

So, to come up with a couple of principles that might help teachers determine if their test-prep activities were helpful or harmful, I carved out the two guidelines you find in the chapter, namely, *professional ethics* and *educational defensibility*. Back then, I called each of these guidelines a "standard." Thus, I urged teachers to use the Educational Defensibility Standard and the Professional Ethics Standard to evaluate the adequacy of any test preparation being provided to their students. But soon thereafter, many educators began using the term "standard" to refer to the content we try to teach children. Accordingly, in an effort to avoid more confusion about the seemingly ubiquitous presence of the term "standard," in the third edition of *Classroom Assessment* I've used the descriptor "guideline" for each of the two *former* standards. I suppose that, to play it safe, I could have called them "things!"

What I wanted to provide teachers with was a couple of points *to think about* when considering the appropriateness of their test-preparation activities. You may be able to come up with better ways to state these two guidelines, or even other factors to consider. I wanted to keep this simple, though. So, because 10 commandments seemed to have worked fairly well I was sure I could get teachers to consider one-fifth that many.

I hope you'll help your students think seriously about this problem area. It's a serious one. In far too many classrooms, kids are being given less-than-appropriate instruction simply because of a teacher's thoughtless test-preparation activities.

Activities

Three activities are proffered for your consideration related to this chapter. The first gives your students more practice in determining how the chapter's two guidelines work by having students generate exemplars or nonexemplars of test-preparation activities, then practice judging whether such examples violate or adhere to one of the guidelines.

The second activity tries to get students to think through just how they would approach a seasoned set of teachers to get them to learn more about test preparation, then translate what new test-preparation insights into the classroom.

The final activity deals with an appraisal of some of the numerous test-preparation materials that now seem to flood the market (and most of them are even accompanied by "money-back" guarantees that, if used, they will raise test scores!).

Chapter Test

For this chapter there's a 10-item True-False test provided. Its statements address most of the chapter's important points, sometimes untruthfully.

Answer Key. 1: T, 2: F, 3: T, 4: T, 5: F, 6: F, 7: T, 8: F, 9: F, 10: F.

Chapter Activities

♦♦♦ Guideline Exemplars/Nonexemplars

Split your class into small groups. Then, assign one of the chapter's two guidelines to a group, alternating so that both guidelines are treated by a sufficient number of groups. Ask each group to prepare written examples—examples that can be read aloud for the rest of the class. Each example should either adhere to the group's designated guideline *or* violate that guideline. Each group should prepare a minimum of five examples, at least one of which adheres or violates the group's guideline. In other words, the examples generated by a group should have at least some variety with respect to adherence/violation of a guideline.

Then, after the groups have developed their examples, randomly select one or two groups for each guideline, and have them read their examples aloud. The rest of the class, individually, notes on scratch paper whether they think the example did or didn't adhere to the guideline being illustrated.

After all of a group's examples have been given, the group should give its own "answer key." Disagreements regarding any group's examples should be discussed by the class, and resolved by you, before moving on to the next group's exemplars/nonexemplars.

♦♦♦ Selection Strategies

The pressure to raise students' test scores is enormous in many locales these days. Suppose you wanted to make certain that teachers really understood the virtues and vices of different sorts of test-preparation practices. Ask small groups of your class to deliberate for 10-15 minutes about how best to get an experienced school faculty to think carefully about the issue of test preparation and, as a result of such thinking, to engage in more appropriate test preparation in their own classes.

Get some or all of the groups to report the essence of the strategies they might use to accomplish this important task. Then see if there are any consensi emerging from your entire class regarding the best ways to get teachers to consider this issue, then personally adhere to more defensible test-preparation practices. (Note the use of the Latin plural, "consensi." I try to make my five years of high school and college Latin pay off, but it's a struggle.)

♦♦♦ Materials Review

A profusion of test-preparation booklets, audiotapes, and videotapes now seems ready to envelop educators who possess the money to buy such products. Early on in the course, ask your students to be on the lookout for such test-preparation materials. Then, when you deal with Chapter 14, ask your students to bring in such materials to see if your class regards them as appropriate.

You might set up small review groups who could each focus on one or two of these products. (Printed materials work best for this activity, but I have occasionally tried it with a test-prep video.) After the reviews are finished, carry out a full-class critique of the test-preparation products you have considered.

CHAPTER 14 TEST

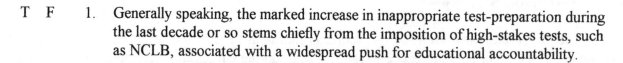

Directions: For each of the following ten statements, based on the chapter's contents, indicate whether the statement is *True* (Circle the T.) or *False* (Circle the F.).

T F 1. Generally speaking, the marked increase in inappropriate test-preparation during the last decade or so stems chiefly from the imposition of high-stakes tests, such as NCLB, associated with a widespread push for educational accountability.

T F 2. The heart of the *Professional Ethics Guideline* is that teachers should not prepare students for tests in a way that violates the canons of fundamental morality.

T F 3. The essence of the *Educational Defensibility Guideline* is that a suitable test-preparation practice will boost students' mastery on both an assessment domain (of knowledge and/or skill) as well as the test representing that domain.

T F 4. Generalized test-taking preparation, if not excessively lengthy, represents an appropriate way to ready students for a high-stakes test.

T F 5. Current-form preparation, that is, special instruction based on an existing form of a test, can be appropriate in some situations.

T F 6. "Teaching to the test," having been employed as a descriptive phrase for so many years by both educators and laypersons, is fairly well understood by most people.

T F 7. A teacher's instruction should be directed toward the body of knowledge and/or skills represented by a test rather than toward the actual items on a test.

T F 8. Most standardized achievement tests are accompanied by fairly explicit descriptions of what is being measured, such descriptions being sufficiently clear for teachers' instructional planning purposes.

T F 9. The use of "clone" items in test-preparation activities is highly recommended because it is consistent with both of the chapter's two test-preparation guidelines.

T F 10. There is, in reality, no truly acceptable way that a teacher can prepare students for a high-stakes test.

CHAPTER 15

EVALUATING TEACHING AND GRADING STUDENTS

Instructor to Instructor

Halting the Harm

Some really bad things are happening in America's classrooms as a direct consequence of educational measurement. I suppose it would be more accurate to say those bad things are happening as a direct consequence of educational *mismeasurement*. I am referring to the unsound instructional activities we see taking place in the classrooms of teachers who are under ever-increasing pressure to raise their students' scores on standardized achievement tests.

Among the most serious effects of this stress on score-boosting are (1) *curricular reductionism* in the sense that many teachers now simply resist teaching students anything not covered in a high-stakes test and (2) *instructional drudgery* wherein teachers force students to engage in relentless test-focused drills designed exclusively to raise test scores, not teach children something they might need to know for a non-test situation. And both of these unfortunate classroom events are directly attributable to a mission most teachers recognize that their administrators want them to carry out, namely, "Raise those test scores!"

I've worried a good deal about the educationally harmful consequences arising from mismeasuring educational quality via standardized achievement tests. As suggested in the chapter, I think that a two-pronged correction strategy just might work. First, teachers need to understand, at more than a slogan-mouthing level, *why* it is inappropriate to judge educational quality by using standardized achievement tests. And, having acquired such an understanding, they need to share it. Second, teachers need to collect solid, credible evidence to show how well they're teaching. I've tried to address both of those points in the chapter. If you think one or both of these two suggestions are reasonable, I hope you can help your students recognize the virtues of this two-pronged approach. If we don't do something to stop this harm-inducing approach to evaluating educational quality, then it most surely will continue—and will continue to reduce the quality of education our children receive.

In the past few years, whenever I teach a classroom assessment course, I make certain that my students understand, at a level solid enough to inform others, just why it is that the use of standardized achievement tests is so unsound. And I give them plenty of practice in word-spreading. For instance, I make certain to incorporate the chapter's first potential activity (to be described a bit later). In that activity my students get *practice* explaining to teachers, parents, or school board members why it is that standardized achievement tests ought not be used to evaluate instructional quality. You can decide, of course, whether you wish to emphasize the acquisition of this "promulgation capacity" on the part of your own students.

Grading's Gunk

The second topic addressed in the chapter is grading. My own purpose in this chapter is to get my students (teachers or teachers-in-training) to accept the inherent imprecision associated with that enterprise. If I can get my students to consider several grade-giving options, and also to recognize that none is infallible, then I'm content. In the current edition of *Classroom Assessment*, I also include a brief treatment of "hodgepodge" grading. I do so because, as I recall my years as a high school teacher, I am convinced that I was a "closet" hodgepodge grader. I was surprised to see the research suggesting that students would rather be hodgepodge-graded than be graded by less multifaceted schemes.

Activities

As indicated above, the initial activity calls for students, in subgroups, to organize their thinking about how to inform colleagues, parents, or policymakers about why standardized achievement tests should not be used to evaluate instructional quality. It usually turns out to be a successful activity in my classes, because students' knowledge of the issue is not only reinforced, but students begin to recognize that "spreading this particular message" is one of their responsibilities.

The second activity will depend on your being able to secure copies of a standardized achievement test, either a currently used form or a previously used form. If you do employ a current test form, of course, be sure to employ appropriate control of any photocopied test forms so that test security is not breached.

The final activity focuses on grade-giving and deals with the fundamental imprecision of teachers' grade-determination efforts.

Chapter Test

A ten-item, short-answer test is supplied for this chapter. When using the answer key presented below, be sure to allow for reasonable paraphrases of the answers provided here.

Answer. 1: Whereas *formative evaluation* focuses on decisions aimed at the improvement of a teacher's ongoing instruction, *summative evaluation* deals with more permanent go/no-go decisions such as termination or the granting of tenure., 2: *Evaluation* deals with the determination of a teacher's instructional effectiveness; *grading* deals with letting students know how well they are performing., 3: The pretest is usually reactive, and this often confounds how students react to the instruction and how they react to the posttest; (or) a different-difficulty pretest and posttest provide difficult-to-interpret evidence of the instruction's impact., 4: This data-gathering design provides (based on a 50 percent sample of a teacher's class) two pretest-to-posttest contrasts using an identical pretest and posttest, but contrasts in which students will not have already seen the posttest they are given., 5: Teaching-testing mismatches signify that a substantial amount of the content contained in the test's items may not have been taught—or may not even supposed to have been taught., 6: Confounded causality arises from the uncertain *cause* of a student's score on a standardized achievement test. That score stems in an unknown degree from the student's socioeconomic status, the student's inherited intellectual aptitudes, and what the student actually learned in school., 7: In order to create a suitable score-spread among test-takers, items with high p values are typically not included in such tests or are subsequently removed at test-revision time. Yet items on which students perform well often cover the content teachers thought important enough to stress. The better students do on an item, the less likely that items covering important, teacher-stressed content will be found on a standardized achievement test., 8: This is a grading system in which students' grades are dependent not on any sort of relative comparisons among students, but on the teacher's predetermined conception of what levels of student quality must be attained for different grades., 9: Relative grading is based on the comparative performances of students *in a given class* so that the level of quality needed for an A in a particular teacher's class may vary substantially from year to year, that is, from class to class., 10: Hodgepodge grading represents the allocation of grades based on a teacher's loosely combined judgments regarding students' assessed achievements, effort, attitudes, in-class conduct, and growth.

Chapter Activities

♦ ♦ ♦ Persuasiveness Wins!

Organize your students into groups of four or more per group, then have each group prepare to give an oral presentation defending the following proposition: "Standardized achievement tests should not be used to evaluate educational quality."

Pick one or more of the following audiences for the groups: (1) educational colleagues, that is, teachers and administrators; (2) parents; and/or (3) educational policymakers such as state legislators or members of district or state boards of education. In other words, you may choose to have each subgroup prepare a presentation for the same audience, or you may assign different target audiences for different subgroups.

After 20 or so minutes of preparation time, choose one of the groups to make their presentation while the other students assume the roles of the target group, for instance, teachers, parents, or board members.

If you have your groups preparing for different audiences, you might choose one group to present to each audience. Otherwise one or, at most, two group presentations should suffice. At the close of the presentation(s), a group-critique of the presentations' strengths and weaknesses is usually illuminating.

♦ ♦ ♦ It's the Items, Stupid!

I often say the name of this activity to myself in recognition of my personal slowness in figuring out that I needed to be spending more time with the actual items on standardized achievement tests. When, a very few years ago, I started going through those items, one at a time, I felt like a genuine dullard for not having devoted serious attention to the actual items in years past. Items illustrate. Items help people understand. Items are the key! *If* you can gain access to a copy of a currently used or formerly used standardized achievement test, your students will be in for a genuine learning experience if you choose to carry out this activity.

First off, you'll need to make copies of a sufficient number of pages from the test. Number the copies so you can be certain to regain all copies—especially if you are using a currently operational form of a standardized achievement test.

Then get your students prepared to carry out an in-class review of the items. (Pick as many items as the available time permits.) Explain to students that the up-coming item review is intended to determine the appropriateness of the test as an indicator of teachers' instructional success. Tell your students their task is not to judge whether they would like children to be able to respond correctly to an item. (We all would.) Rather, for each item they are to make two individual judgments:

- Is a prominent determiner of a student's success on this item a child's *socioeconomic status* or the education level of the child's parents? *Yes or No?*

- Is a prominent determiner of a student's success on this item *inherited academic aptitudes* such as a child's in-born verbal, quantitative, or spatial capacities? *Yes or No?*

Then ask your students to review, individually and silently, each of the items you present to them. (Items can also be presented, in group-paced fashion, via an overhead projector. I find that this sometimes works even better than using an items-on-paper approach.) Students make their *two* Yes/No judgments for each item (on scratch paper or on a response form you provide) until about 8-12 items have been reviewed. Then go back and, after getting a per-item tally for each item, discuss the items in relation to the two item-review questions.

I've used this activity with a number of classes. It usually turned out to be one of the most illuminating and one of the most emotionally impactful sessions of the entire course. Your students will simply not believe what they find if you use items from one of the five major nationally standardized achievement tests. It is an eye-opening experience. And, as I continue to say to myself when I wrap up this activity, "See, it surely was the items, stupid!"

♦♦♦ Not Totally Mushy, But Close!

This final activity asks you to split your class into groups again, then ask each group to prepare a 5-10 minute persuasive speech to be given to a group of teacher-education students who are just about to begin their student-teaching assignments. The title of the speech is: "Grade-Giving Isn't As Precise As You May Think!"

After a 15 to 20 minute preparation period, select one or two groups to give their speeches to the rest of the class. At the time, your other class members assume the role of teacher-education students. A brief post-presentation critique of the speech's strengths and weaknesses should follow.

CHAPTER 15 TEST

Directions: In the spaces provided, please supply accurate responses to the questions below.

1. When evaluating a teacher's instruction, what is the difference between *formative evaluation* and *summative evaluation*?

_____

_____

_____

_____

2. Although many people use the terms "grading" and "evaluation" as though the two words are synonymous, what is the technical difference between these two terms?

_____

_____

_____

_____

3. What is *one* reason that a simple one-group, pretest-posttest design will rarely yield convincing evidence of a teacher's instructional effectiveness?

_____

_____

_____

_____

4. What is *one* reason that the "split-and-switch" design can provide believable evidence of a teacher's instructional effectiveness?

_____

_____

_____

_____

5. It is said that one reason students' standardized achievement test scores should not be used to evaluate instruction is that there is a "teaching-testing mismatch." What does this mean?

_____

_____

_____

_____

6. When standardized achievement tests are rejected as suitable measures to use for evaluating teaching because of "confounded causality," what does this mean?

_____

_____

_____

_____

7. What does it mean when the use of standardized achievement tests is rejected because of these tests' "technical tendency to exclude items covering important content?"

    _____
    _____
    _____
    _____

8. What is meant by *absolute grading*?

    _____
    _____
    _____
    _____

9. What is *relative grading*?

    _____
    _____
    _____
    _____

10. What is meant by the expression, *hodgepodge grading*?

    _____
    _____
    _____
    _____

MID-COURSE EXAMINATION

Directions: Select the *best* response for each of the following items. Some of the items ask you to identify one of the item's four choices that is *not* in the same category as the other three choices. In such instances, the *not* in the item's stem will always be italicized.

1. Which of the following is *not* a traditionally cited reason that classroom teachers need to know about assessment?

   A. So teachers can monitor students' progress.
   B. So teachers can assign grades to students.
   C. So teachers can diagnose students' strengths and weaknesses.
   D. So teachers can clarify their instructional intentions.

2. A history teacher, Mrs. Scroggins, tries to determine the consistency of her tests by occasionally re-administering them to her students, then seeing how much similarity there was in the way her students performed. What kind of reliability evidence is Mrs. Scroggins attempting to collect?

   A. Stability
   B. Alternate form
   C. Internal consistency
   D. None of the above

3. Which of the following statements best describes the relationship among the three sanctioned forms of reliability evidence?

   A. All three types of evidence are essentially equivalent.
   B. Stability reliability evidence is more important than either internal-consistency evidence or alternate-form evidence.
   C. The three forms of evidence represent fundamentally different ways of representing a test's consistency.
   D. The three forms of evidence differ in their significance because internal-consistency evidence of a test's reliability is a necessary condition for the other two types of consistency.

4. Test-retest data regarding assessment consistency is an instance of:

   A. Stability reliability
   B. Alternate-form reliability
   C. Internal-consistency reliability
   D. None of the above

5. The *standard error of measurement* is focused chiefly on:

   A. Construct-related evidence of validity
   B. Content-related evidence of validity
   C. Criterion-related evidence of validity
   D. None of the above

6. Intervention studies, differential-population studies, and related-measures studies are all instances of ways to collect:

   A. Content-related evidence of validity
   B. Criterion-related evidence of validity
   C. Construct-related evidence of validity
   D. None of the above

7. Which one of the following statements *could* be technically correct?

   A. "The test-based inference is valid."
   B. "The test is definitely valid."
   C. "The test is face-valid."
   D. "The test is consequentially valid."

8. Classroom teachers are most apt to focus on which of the following?

   A. Evidence of alternate-form reliability
   B. Criterion-related evidence of validity
   C. Evidence of internal-consistency reliability
   D. Content-related evidence of validity

9. What kind of evidence is most eagerly sought by the commercial testing firms that develop *academic aptitude* tests?

   A. Criterion-related evidence of validity
   B. Evidence that a test is thought to be face-valid
   C. Content-related evidence of validity
   D. Evidence that the consequences of a test's use will be positive

10. What should be the two major concerns of a classroom teacher who wishes to eliminate bias in the teacher's assessment instruments?

    A. Unfair penalization and reliability of items in the teacher's tests
    B. Offensiveness and absence-of-bias in items in the teacher's tests
    C. Offensiveness and unfair penalization of items in the teacher's tests
    D. Disparate impact and offensiveness of items in the teacher's tests

11. Which of the following is typically recommended for use with students who have the most serious disabilities?

   A.   Alternate assessments
   B.   Assessment accommodations
   C.   No assessments whatsoever
   D.   Regular assessments

12. Which of the following views regarding the assessment of limited-English proficient (LEP) students is most defensible?

   A.   LEP students, if tested with regular English-language tests, will often outperform students whose native language is English.
   B.   The use of assessment accommodations for LEP students typically leads to more valid test-based inferences about those students.
   C.   It is relatively easy to develop alternate tests for LEP students in those students' native languages.
   D.   Almost all groups charged with the assessment of LEP students urge the use either of translated tests or, failing that, the provision of interpreters for LEP students.

13. What kind of instructional objective is Mrs. Jenkins pursuing when she wants her students to become able to distinguish between facts and opinions presented in a newspaper's "Letters to the Editor?"

   A.   Cognitive
   B.   Affective
   C.   Psychomotor
   D.   None of the above

14. As most educators currently use the expression, "content standard," to which of the following is that phrase most equivalent?

   A.   The level of proficiency sought for students
   B.   A performance standard
   C.   Content-related evidence of validity
   D.   An instructional objective

15. Which of the following statements is most accurate?

   A.   A test built to provide norm-referenced inferences about students is likely to yield accurate criterion-referenced inferences about those students.
   B.   A test built to provide criterion-referenced inferences about students can also be used to make defensible norm-referenced inferences about those students.
   C.   Norm-referenced inferences and criterion-referenced inferences about students are essentially interchangeable.
   D.   Criterion-referenced tests and norm-referenced tests, that is, the assessment instruments themselves, are not fundamentally different.

16. Which of the following is *not* a type of selected-response assessment item?

   A. A matching item
   B. A multiple binary-choice item
   C. A short-answer item
   D. A binary-choice item

17. Which of the following represents the most synonymous label for NCLB's designation of "student academic achievement standards?"

   A. Academic content standards
   B. Curricular goals
   C. Adequate yearly progress
   D. Performance standards

18. The National Assessment of Educational Progress (NAEP):

   A. is a mandatory examination in reading and mathematics that must be taken annually by a sample of students in each state.
   B. was first established in 1996 by the U.S. Congress to serve as an accountability oriented nation's "report card."
   C. assesses national samples of U.S. students at three grade levels every few years in academic subjects.
   D. sets forth prescribed assessment frameworks at three grade levels, such frameworks to be followed by the 50 states in framing their own state content standards.

19. Which of the following is *not* a general item-writing rule that is applicable to the creation of items for all classroom assessments?

   A. Do not provide unclear directions to students about how to respond to an assessment.
   B. Do not inform students about how much the items on a test will be weighted.
   C. Do not employ sentence-structures unlikely to be easily understood by students.
   D. Do not employ words, phrases, or sentences apt to be regarded as ambiguous to students.

20. Which of the following is *not* a recommended item-writing rule for the creation of binary-choice items?

   A. Include only a single concept in any statement.
   B. Phrase items so that a superficial analysis by students will suggest an incorrect answer.
   C. Rarely use statements containing double negatives, although single negatives are acceptable.
   D. Keep item length similar for both of the binary categories being assessed.

21. Which of the following conclusions regarding multiple binary-choice items has *not* been supported by available research?

   A. These items are highly efficient in gathering student achievement data.
   B. These items are a bit less difficult for students than multiple-choice items.
   C. These items tend to be more reliable than other forms of selected-response items.
   D. These items are regarded by students as more difficult than multiple-choice items.

22. Of the following four statements, one is *not* a guideline to be followed when constructing multiple-choice items. Which statement is it?

   A. Randomly assign correct answers to the available answer-choice positions.
   B. To keep stems brief, place most words in an item's alternatives.
   C. Don't let the length of alternatives suggest correct or incorrect answers.
   D. Never use "all of the above" as a response option.

23. Which of the following is a generally recommended item-writing rule for matching items?

   A. Whenever possible, employ heterogeneous lists of premises and responses.
   B. Typically, employ more premises than responses, allowing each response to be used more than once.
   C. Employ relatively long lists, usually containing at least two-dozen premises or responses.
   D. In the test's directions, describe the basis for matching and the number of times a response can be used.

24. Presented below are four item-writing rules. Which one is a guideline often recommended for the construction of short-answer items?

   A. Typically employ direct questions rather than incomplete statements, especially for young students.
   B. For incomplete statements, use at least three blanks, preferably more.
   C. Be certain that the length of a blank coincides roughly with the correct answer's likely length.
   D. Structure an item, both verbally and in format, so that students can decide how lengthy their response should be.

25. Select the one *accurate* guideline below for teachers who are scoring students' responses to essay items.

   A. Early on during the scoring process, depending on students' responses, decide how much weight you should give to the mechanics of writing.
   B. Be sure that your students identify their own essay responses clearly so you can take students' aptitudes into consideration.
   C. Prepare at least a tentative scoring key in advance of judging students' responses to any item.
   D. Score every student's response using two approaches: first holistically, then analytically.

FINAL EXAMINATION

> Directions: Select the *best* response for each of the following items. Some of the items ask you to identify one of the item's four choices that is *not* in the same category as the other three choices. In such instances, the *not* in the item's stem will always be italicized.

1. Which of the following statements most accurately reflects the relationship between students' aptitude and their achievement?

    A. Both aptitude and achievement are equivalent to a traditional conception of intelligence.
    B. Whereas aptitude tends to reflect potential, achievement tends to reflect prior learning.
    C. Actually, achievement is little more than an operationalization of aptitude.
    D. The level of a student's aptitude can never exceed the level of the student's achievement.

2. If Mr. Higgins, a fourth-grade teacher, tries to evaluate his major exams by ascertaining the degree to which his test's items are functioning in a similar manner, what kind of test-evaluative evidence is this?

    A. Stability reliability evidence
    B. Alternate-form reliability evidence
    C. Internal-consistency reliability evidence
    D. None of the above

3. How does "classification consistency" differ conceptually from more traditional indicators of test reliability?

    A. Classification-consistency approaches are focused more on categorizing students' performances unchangingly rather than supplying only numerical indices of consistency.
    B. Classification-consistency approaches do not employ numerical indicators of an assessment's consistency, unlike traditional reliability procedures.
    C. In contrast to traditional reliability approaches, if there are no actual decisions linked to a test's use, it is impossible to determine a test's classification consistency.
    D. Whereas the three traditional forms of reliability evidence are largely interchangeable, classification-consistency approaches to reliability are truly distinctive.

4. Cronbach's *coefficient alpha* and the Kuder-Richardson reliability formulae are examples of:

    A. Stability coefficients
    B. Alternate-form coefficients
    C. Internal-consistency coefficients
    D. None of the above

5. Which of the following is the most useful indicator of the consistency of an individual student's test performance?

A. A polytomous item-analysis
B. A dichotomous item-analysis
C. A standard error of measurement
D. An alternate-form reliability coefficient

6. Which of the following is a typical classroom teacher most likely to collect?

A. Content-related evidence of validity
B. Predictive criterion-related evidence of validity
C. Concurrent criterion-related evidence of validity
D. Standard-error-of-measurement evidence

7. Which of the following approaches to assessment validity is the most intuitively incomprehensible?

A. Content-related strategies
B. Criterion-related strategies
C. Construct-related strategies
D. There are no comprehensibility differences among the three assessment validation strategies.

8. Which of the following descriptions of validity is most accurate?

A. Validity refers to the consistency with which a test measures whatever it is measuring.
B. Validity describes the degree to which a test's usage leads to appropriate consequences for examinees.
C. Validity describes the legitimacy of the decision to which a test-based inference will be put.
D. Validity refers to the accuracy of score-based interpretations about examinees.

9. Differential-population studies, related-measures studies, and intervention studies are chiefly associated with which of the following?

A. Content-related evidence of validity
B. Criterion-related evidence of validity
C. Construct-related evidence of validity
D. None of the above

10. Which of the following assertions most accurately captures the relationship between *disparate impact* of a test and *assessment bias*?

A. If a test has a disparate impact on different student subgroups, the test is *a priori* biased.
B. If a test is biased, it will only rarely have a disparate impact on different student subgroups.
C. A test that is biased against either gender group will almost certainly be biased against ethnic groups.
D. If a test has a disparate impact on different student subgroups, the test is not necessarily biased.

11. *Differential item functioning* (DIF) is employed in connection with which of the following approaches to bias-detection?

A. Empirical approaches
B. Judgmental approaches
C. Both empirical and judgmental approaches
D. Neither empirical nor judgmental approaches

12. Which of the following approaches to bias-elimination is it most reasonable to expect classroom teachers to use?

A. Empirical approaches
B. Judgmental approaches
C. Both empirical and judgmental approaches are equally reasonable for classroom teachers to use.
D. Neither empirical nor judgmental approaches are reasonable for classroom teachers to use.

13. What sort of instructional outcome is Mr. Bevins seeking to accomplish when he wants his biology students to "develop a sincere respect for the scientific process?"

A. Cognitive
B. Affective
C. Psychomotor
D. None of the above

14. As employed by most of today's educators, to which of the following is the expression, "content standard" most equivalent?

A. Performance standard
B. Content validity
C. Educational objective
D. Curricular assessment

15. Which of the following assertions is most accurate?

    A. Criterion-referenced score-based inferences are absolute interpretations.
    B. Norm-referenced score-based inferences are absolute interpretations.
    C. Norm-referenced score-based inferences and criterion-referenced score-based inferences are essentially interchangeable.
    D. Norm-referenced score-based inferences are typically more useful to classroom teachers than criterion-referenced score-based inferences.

16. Which of the following is *not* a type of constructed-response item?

    A. A matching item
    B. A fill-in-the-blanks item
    C. An essay item
    D. A short-answer item

17. The accountability provisions of the *No Child Left Behind Act* call for schools and districts to make "adequate yearly progress" by annually increasing the proportion of students scoring at least which one of the following levels on a state's NCLB tests?

    A. Advanced
    B. Proficient
    C. Basic
    D. Below Basic

18. What is the chief role of the National Assessment of Educational Progress (NAEP)?

    A. To compare the academic performances of U.S. students with those of students in other nations
    B. To promote more consistent curriculum targets in the 50 U.S. states
    C. To monitor U.S. students' academic achievement over time
    D. To satisfy the measurement requirements of any state whose officials wish to measure students' mastery of specific content standards

19. Which of the following is a general item-writing rule that should be followed in the writing of all items for classroom assessments?

    A. To challenge students adequately, use vocabulary terms slightly more advanced than required.
    B. If possible, provide clues for students to come up with correct answers even if those clues are not directly relevant to the knowledge and/or skill being assessed.
    C. Because stronger students will usually be able to discern the nature of the assessment tasks before them, directions about how students are to respond need not be specific or detailed.
    D. Attempt to employ syntax in test items that is well within the understanding levels of the students being assessed.

20. Which of the following is a recommended item-writing rule for the construction of binary-choice items?

   A. Include no more than two concepts in any one statement.
   B. Employ a roughly equal number of statements representing the two categories being tested.
   C. If one category being assessed requires longer statements than the other category, be sure that the disparity in statement-length is constant.
   D. Employ relatively few double-negative statements and, if you do, be sure to emphasize with italics or bold-face type that a negative is involved.

21. One of the important rules to be followed in creating multiple binary-choice items is that:

   A. Most items should mesh sensibly with a cluster's stimulus material.
   B. Item clusters should be strikingly separated from one another.
   C. The stimulus material for any cluster of items should contain a substantial amount of extraneous information.
   D. Multiple binary-choice items, to avoid confusion, should never be included in a test already containing binary-choice items.

22. Which of the following is an item-writing guideline for the construction of multiple-choice items?

   A. Generally, especially with young children, the stem should consist of an incomplete statement rather than direct question.
   B. Don't ever use "all-of-the-above" alternatives, but use a "none-of-the-above" alternative to increase an item's difficulty.
   C. Typically, make the later answer options, such as "C" and "D," the correct answers.
   D. Supply clues to the correct answer by using alternatives of dissimilar lengths.

23. Which of the following rules is often recommended for the generation of matching items?

   A. Order all of the premises alphabetically, but arrange the responses in an unpredictable manner.
   B. Place the premises for an item on one page, then put most of the responses for that item on the following page.
   C. Ideally, both the premises and the responses should represent fundamentally heterogeneous lists.
   D. Employ relatively brief lists, placing the shorter words or phrases at the right.

24. One of the following rules for the construction of essay items is accurate. The other three rules are not. Which is the correct rule?

    A.   Force students to allocate their time judiciously by never indicating how much time should be expended on a particular item.
    B.   Give students an opportunity to match their achievement levels with the essay test by allowing them to choose, from optional items, those they will answer.
    C.   Construct all essay items so that the student's task for each item is unambiguously described.
    D.   Judge the quality of a given set of essay items by seeing how accurately a tryout group of students can comprehend what responses are sought.

25. Which of the rules given below accurately reflects one of the guidelines generally given to classroom teachers who must score students' responses to essay items?

    A.   Score an entire test, that is, the student's responses to all items, before going on to the next student's test.
    B.   After all answers to all essay items have been scored, decide how much weight you should give—if any—to such factors as spelling, punctuation, and grammar.
    C.   Attempt to apply Bloom's Cognitive Taxonomy to the scoring process.
    D.   Prepare a tentative scoring key prior to judging any student's response—being ready to modify it if this seems warranted during the scoring.

26. Which of the following is *not* an element typically embodied in performance tests?

    A.   Judgmental appraisal of students' responses
    B.   Prespecified evaluative criteria for judging students' responses
    C.   Multiple evaluative criteria
    D.   A direct link to a preexisting content standard

27. Which of the following would be the most suitable assessment target for a Likert inventory?

    A.   Students' attitudes toward selves as learners
    B.   Students' ability to write a self-illuminating essay about themselves
    C.   Students' skill in solving complex geometric problems
    D.   Students' abilities to perform routine physical skills such as ball-tossing and ball-catching

28. Consider the following set of factors that could be employed to judge the quality of the tasks for performance tests. Which one is *not* generally endorsed as a task-selection factor?

    A.   Motivational impact on students
    B.   Authenticity
    C.   Teachability of the skill assessed by a task
    D.   Feasibility of implementation

29. A *rubric* is a scoring guide to be employed in judging students' responses to constructed-response assessments such as a performance test. Which one of the following elements is the *least* necessary feature of a properly constructed rubric?

   A. An identification of the evaluative criteria to be used in appraising a student's response
   B. A designation of a performance standard that is required for skill-mastery
   C. Descriptions of different quality levels associated with each evaluative criterion
   D. An indication of whether a holistic or analytic scoring approach is to be used

30. Which of the following phrases is most commonly used to describe a portfolio focused on a student's self-evaluative and ongoing improvement in the quality of work products?

   A. Working portfolio
   B. Showcase portfolio
   C. Formative portfolio
   D. Summative portfolio

31. Which of the following is *not* a key step that a classroom teacher needs to take in getting underway with a portfolio assessment program?

   A. Decide on the kinds of work samples to collect.
   B. Decide which students should be involved in the portfolio assessment program.
   C. Require students to evaluate continually their own portfolio products.
   D. Schedule and conduct a meaningful number of portfolio conferences.

32. Which of the following, from a classroom teacher's perspective, is probably the most serious drawback of portfolio assessment?

   A. Parents' negative reactions to portfolio assessment
   B. Students' negative reactions to portfolio assessment
   C. Portfolio assessment's time-demands on teachers
   D. The excessive attention given to portfolio assessment by educational policymakers

33. Many experienced assessors of student affect suggest that the most appropriate way for classroom teachers to monitor their students' affect is through the use of:

   A. Anonymously completed self-report inventories
   B. Anonymously completed personalized essays
   C. Teacher observations of affect-related student behaviors
   D. Affectively oriented performance tests

34. Which of the following is the *most* troublesome problem facing those educators who wish to rely heavily on the use of performance tests?

   A. Generating tasks for performance tests
   B. Scoring students' responses to a performance test's task(s)
   C. Making valid inferences about students' generalized skill-mastery
   D. Persuading students to respond seriously to a performance test's task(s)

35. Which of the following is *not* an important rule to be followed in the classroom assessment of student affect?

    A. Make all inferences about students' affective status so that the inferences are group-focused rather than individual-focused.
    B. If any self-report inventories are used, students' responses must be truly anonymous.
    C. Any affective variable being measured must be genuinely noncontroversial.
    D. To monitor students' ever-changing attitudes and interests, assess affect on at least a bi-weekly basis.

36. Which of the following steps is *not* one that should be followed in the creation of a Likert inventory for use in classroom assessment?

    A. Generate a series of favorable and unfavorable statements regarding the affective variable being measured.
    B. Have several reviewers classify each statement as positive or negative, then discard any statement that most reviewers do not agree with your classifications.
    C. Administer the inventory to your own students or, as a tryout, to another teacher's students.
    D. Identify and eliminate statements that, upon the basis of the tryout, function differently than the other statements.

37. Which of the following contentions about affective assessment in the classroom is *not* accurate?

    A. If classroom affective assessment is introduced, it invariably diminishes the attention given to the measurement of higher-level cognitive outcomes.
    B. Classroom affective assessment typically focuses a teacher's instructional concerns more directly on the promotion of affective objectives for students.
    C. Anonymity enhancement procedures for classroom affective assessment are extremely desirable.
    D. If affective assessment is to take place in classrooms, many teachers will need to learn about affect-focused instructional techniques.

38. If classroom teachers set out to improve their own tests using judgmental approaches, which of the following review criteria is *not* a factor that teachers ought to consider?

    A. Adherence to item-specific guidelines and general item-writing rules
    B. Absence of any significant gaps in a test's content coverage
    C. Each item's likely contribution to a valid score-based inference about a student's status
    D. The likelihood that, if a test is seen by parents, those parents will recognize the suitability of an item's content coverage

39. Which of the following indices represents an item's difficulty?

    A. *p* value
    B. Correlation coefficient
    C. Discrimination index
    D. Distractor efficiency

40. For tests intended to provide norm-referenced interpretations, which of the following kinds of items should be sought?

   A. Negative discriminators
   B. Positive discriminators
   C. Nondiscriminators
   D. None of the above

41. Which one of the following statements regarding the improvement of classroom assessments is *not* accurate?

   A. Classroom teachers can employ judgmental improvement procedures, empirical procedures, or both.
   B. For selected-response tests, especially multiple-choice items, distractor analyses can prove useful in item-improvement.
   C. Performance-based approaches to item improvement usually are different for tests aimed at criterion-referenced inferences than for those aimed at norm-referenced inferences.
   D. Students' reactions to test items should play little or no role in item improvement.

42. Which of the following questions is *not* answered more suitably by using the results of classroom assessments?

   A. What to teach?
   B. How to teach it?
   C. How long to teach it?
   D. How well was it taught?

43. If a classroom test is constructed prior to a teacher's instructional planning, there are potential dividends that follow. Which of the following is *not* an instructional advantage that stems from the creation of classroom tests prior to instructional planning?

   A. A teacher's more accurate task analyses
   B. A teacher's provision of more on-target practice for students
   C. More lucid explanations by the teacher
   D. More defensible allocation of students' grades

44. Which of the following is an *instructionally* beneficial rubric?

   A. Task-specific rubric
   B. Hypergeneral rubric
   C. Skill-focused rubric
   D. None of the above

45. Which of the following rules is *not* one that is recommended when creating a scoring rubric that will have a positive impact on classroom instruction?

    A.   Make certain the skill to be assessed is truly significant.

    B.   Be sure that all of the rubric's evaluative criteria can be addressed instructionally by teachers.

    C.   Employ as many evaluative criteria as possible to judge major aspects of students' responses.

    D.   Provide a terse label for each of the rubric's evaluative criteria.

46. Which of the following is the *most* often misinterpreted score-interpretation indicator used with standardized tests?

    A.   Raw score

    B.   Percentile

    C.   Stanine

    D.   Grade-equivalent score

47. Consider the following statements regarding test-preparation. Which one is *not* accurate?

    A.   Appropriate test-preparation will simultaneously improve students' test scores as well as students' mastery of the knowledge and/or skills represented by the test.

    B.   If relatively brief, generalized test-taking preparation focused on such skills as how to manage one's time during test-taking is quite appropriate.

    C.   If teachers simultaneously direct their instruction toward a test's specific items and the content domain on which the test is based, this constitutes appropriate test preparation.

    D.   If teachers adhere to the ethical norms of the education profession while preparing their students, this is an important ingredient in appropriate test-preparation activities.

48. Which of these four test-preparation practices is the *least* appropriate?

    A.   Previous-form preparation

    B.   Current-form preparation

    C.   Same-format preparation

    D.   Varied-format preparation

49. Which of the following reasons is *not* one that should disincline policymakers to evaluate educational quality primarily on the basis of students' scores on standardized achievement tests?

    A.   There are often substantial mismatches between the content covered on such tests and local curricular emphases.

    B.   Substantial gaps between minority and majority students' performance on such tests are often found.

    C.   There is a technical tendency to remove from such tests items covering important, teacher-stressed knowledge and skills.

    D.   It is difficult to tell from such tests how much of a student's test performance is due to what was taught in school rather than to students' socioeconomic status or inherited academic aptitudes.

50.   Which of the following statements about grading is most defensible?

A.   "Hodgepodge grading, although widely practiced, is regarded with considerable disfavor by students."
B.   "If teachers take a number of evaluative factors into consideration, they can usually come up with extremely accurate grades for their students."
C.   "Over the course of a student's school experiences, teachers' too-stringent grades are often balanced out by teachers' too-lenient grades."
D.   "Given the same evaluative data for particular students, most teachers will arrive at identical grades for any given student."

ANSWER KEYS

MID-COURSE EXAMINATION

1. D
2. A
3. C
4. A
5. D
6. C
7. A
8. D
9. A
10. C
11. A
12. B
13. A
14. D
15. B
16. C
17. D
18. C
19. B
20. C
21. B
22. B
23. D
24. A
25. C

FINAL EXAMINATION

1. B
2. C
3. A
4. C
5. C
6. A
7. C
8. D
9. C
10. D
11. A
12. B
13. B
14. C
15. A
16. A
17. B
18. C
19. D
20. B
21. B
22. B
23. D
24. C
25. D
26. D
27. A
28. A
29. B
30. A
31. B
32. C
33. A
34. C
35. D
36. B
37. A
38. D
39. A
40. B
41. D
42. B
43. D
44. C
45. C
46. D
47. C
48. B
49. B
50. C

AN EDUCATIONAL ASSESSMENT CONFIDENCE INVENTORY

Directions: This inventory is intended to determine how confident classroom teachers are regarding the kinds of assessment-related activities they may be called on to carry out. *Anonymously,* please indicate your level of confidence if *you* were asked to carry out the assessment activities described in the inventory. Circle one of the following responses for each activity:

VC =	**FC =**	**LC =**	**NC =**
Very Confident	*Fairly Confident*	*A Little Confident*	*Not Confident At All*

After responding, please return your completed inventory as directed.

Suppose *you* were asked to:	How confident would *you* be?			
1. explain to a group of first-year teachers what is meant by the expression "measurement validity."	VC	FC	LC	NC
2. make a brief presentation at a faculty meeting on the topic: "Why Today's Teacher Needs To Know About Assessment."	VC	FC	LC	NC
3. give a parent at least three solid reasons that a school staff's instructional effectiveness ought not be judged on the basis of students' scores on standardized achievement tests.	VC	FC	LC	NC
4. describe to a group of experienced teachers two guidelines so that their in-class preparation for high-stakes tests would be defensible.	VC	FC	LC	NC
5. tell a friend how a teacher can use a judgmental approach to reduce the amount of assessment bias likely to be present in classroom tests.	VC	FC	LC	NC
6. classify a set of 40 instructional objectives according to whether they are chiefly cognitive, affective, or psychomotor in nature.	VC	FC	LC	NC
7. explain to a school board what the general nature is of Bloom's Taxonomy of Cognitive Objectives.	VC	FC	LC	NC
8. write a brief explanatory note for a monthly district newspaper explaining the key differences between norm-referenced and criterion-referenced interpretations of students' test performances.	VC	FC	LC	NC

Please turn over ☞ ☞ ☞

Suppose *you* were asked to:	**How confident would *you* be?**			
9. for a classroom test, construct a binary-choice item that violates no established guidelines for constructing such items.	VC	FC	LC	NC
10. for a classroom test, construct a multiple binary-choice item that violates no established guidelines for constructing such items.	VC	FC	LC	NC
11. for a classroom test, construct a matching item that violates no established guidelines for constructing such items.	VC	FC	LC	NC
12. for a classroom test, construct a multiple-choice item that violates no established guidelines for constructing such items.	VC	FC	LC	NC
13. for a classroom test, construct a short-answer item that violates no established guidelines for constructing such items.	VC	FC	LC	NC
14. for a classroom test, construct an essay item that violates no established guidelines for constructing such items.	VC	FC	LC	NC
15. for a classroom test, construct a performance test item that violates no established guidelines for constructing such items.	VC	FC	LC	NC
16. for a classroom test, construct a Likert self-report inventory (to assess students' affect) that violates no established guidelines for constructing such inventories.	VC	FC	LC	NC
17. organize and implement a portfolio assessment program for a classroom.	VC	FC	LC	NC
18. construct a scoring rubric that would help a teacher make better instructional decisions.	VC	FC	LC	NC
19. explain to a group of experienced teachers how well-conceived assessment can improve the quality of their instructional decision-making.	VC	FC	LC	NC
20. explain to parents how to interpret the score-report for their child's performance on a nationally standardized achievement test.	VC	FC	LC	NC

Thank you for completing this inventory.

Teaching Tips for First-time Instructors and Adjunct Professors

Teaching Tips Contents

1. How to be an Effective Teacher
Seven principles of good teaching practice
Tips for Thriving: Creating an Inclusive Classroom

2. Today's Undergraduate Students
Traditional students
Nontraditional students
Emerging influences
What students want from college professors
Tips for Thriving: Be a "Facilitator of Learning"

3. Planning Your Course
Constructing the syllabus
Problems to avoid
Tips for Thriving: Visual Quality

4. Your First Class
Seven goals for a successful first meeting
Tips for Thriving: An Icebreaker

5. Strategies for Teaching and Learning
Getting participation through active learning
Team learning
Tips for Thriving: Active Learning and Lecturing

6. Grading and Assessment Techniques
Philosophy of grading
Criterion grading
Tips for Thriving: Result Feedback

7. Using Technology
Advice on using the web in small steps
Tips for Thriving: Using Videos

8. Managing Problem Situations
Cheating
Unmotivated students
Credibility problems
Tips for Thriving: Discipline

9. Surviving When You're Not Prepared
Contingency plans

10. Improving Your Performance
Self evaluation
Tips for Thriving: Video-Recording Your Class

1   How to be an Effective Teacher

(Adapted from Royse, *Teaching Tips for College and University Instructors: A Practical Guide*, published by Allyn & Bacon, Boston, MA, ©2001, by Pearson Education)

A look at 50 years of research "on the way teachers teach and learners learn" reveals seven broad principles of good teaching practice (Chickering and Gamson, 1987).

1. Frequent student-faculty contact: Faculty who are concerned about their students and their progress and who are perceived to be easy to talk to, serve to motivate and keep students involved. Things you can do to apply this principle:

- ✓ Attend events sponsored by students.
- ✓ Serve as a mentor or advisor to students.
- ✓ Keep "open" or "drop-in" office hours.

2. The encouragement of cooperation among students: There is a wealth of research indicating that students benefit from the use of small group and peer learning instructional approaches. Things you can do to apply this principle:

- ✓ Have students share in class their interests and backgrounds.
- ✓ Create small groups to work on projects together.
- ✓ Encourage students to study together.

3. Active learning techniques: Students don't learn much by sitting in the classroom listening; they must talk about what they are learning, write about it, relate to it, and apply it to their lives. Things you can do to apply this principle:

- ✓ Give students actual problems or situations to analyze.
- ✓ Use role-playing, simulations or hands-on experiments.
- ✓ Encourage students to challenge ideas brought into class.

4. Prompt feedback: Learning theory research has consistently shown that the quicker the feedback, the greater the learning. Things you can do to apply this principle:

- ✓ Return quizzes and exams by the next class meeting.
- ✓ Return homework within one week.
- ✓ Provide students with detailed comments on their written papers.

5. Emphasize time on task: This principle refers to the amount of actual involvement with the material being studied and applies, obviously, to the way the instructor uses classroom instructional time. Faculty need good time-management skills. Things you can do to apply this principle:

- ✓ Require students who miss classes to make up lost work.
- ✓ Require students to rehearse before making oral presentations.
- ✓ Don't let class breaks stretch out too long.

6. Communicating high expectations: The key here is not to make the course impossibly difficult, but to have goals that can be attained as long as individual learners stretch and work hard, going beyond what they already know. Things you can do to apply this principle:

- ✓ Communicate your expectations orally and in writing at the beginning of the course.
- ✓ Explain the penalties for students who turn work in late.
- ✓ Identify excellent work by students; display exemplars if possible.

7. Respecting diverse talents and ways of learning: Within any classroom there will be students who have latent talents and some with skills and abilities far beyond any that you might imagine. Understanding your students as individuals and showing regard for their unique talents is "likely to

facilitate student growth and development in every sphere – academic, social, personal, and vocational" (Sorcinelli, 1991, p.21). Things you can do to apply this principle:
- ✓ Use diverse teaching approaches.
- ✓ Allow students some choice of readings and assignments.
- ✓ Try to find out students' backgrounds and interests.

 Tips for Thriving: Creating an Inclusive Classroom

How do you model an open, accepting attitude within your classroom where students will feel it is safe to engage in give-and-take discussions? Firstly, view students as individuals instead of representatives of separate and distinct groups. Cultivate a climate that is respectful of diverse viewpoints, and don't allow ridicule, defamatory or hurtful remarks. Try to encourage everyone in the class to participate, and be alert to showing favoritism.

---

2   Today's Undergraduate Students

(Adapted from: Lyons et al, *The Adjunct Professor's Guide to Success*, published by Allyn & Bacon, Boston, MA, ©1999, by Pearson Education)

Total enrollment in all forms of higher education has increased over 65% in the last thirty years. Much of this increase was among part-time students who now comprise over 70% of total college enrollment. The number of "nontraditional" students, typically defined as 25 years of age or older, has been growing more rapidly than the number of "traditional" students, those under 25 years of age. Though there is a great deal of common ground between students of any age, there are some key differences between younger and older students.

Traditional students: Much more than in previous generations, traditional students are the products of dysfunctional families and have had a less effective primary and secondary education. Traditional students have been conditioned by the aftermath of high-profile ethical scandals (such as Watergate), creating a mindset of cynicism and lack of respect for authority figures – including college professors. Students of this generation are quick to proclaim their "rights". Many of today's students perceive professors as service providers, class attendance as a matter of individual choice, and grades as "pay" to which they are entitled for meeting standards they perceive as reasonable.

Nontraditional students: Many older students are attending college after a long lay-off, frequently doubting their ability to succeed. The other time-consuming challenges in their lives – children, work, caring for aging parents – often prevent adequate preparation for class or contribute to frequent absences. While traditional students demand their "rights," many older students won't ask for the smallest extra consideration (e.g., to turn a project in a few days late). Most older students learn best by doing, by applying the theory of the textbook to the rich set of experiences they have accumulated over the years.

Emerging influences: Today, a fourth of all undergraduate students are members of minority groups. Obviously, ethnicity, language, religion, culture, and sexual orientation are each significant issues to which a professor should be sensitive. The successful professor sees these differences as an opportunity rather than a threat to learning.

 Tips for Thriving: Be a "Facilitator of Learning"

Be energized by students who "don't get it" rather than judgmental of their shortcomings. View yourself as a "facilitator of learning" rather than a "sage on a stage."

What students want from college professors: While each student subgroup has particular characteristics that affect the dynamics of a college learning environment, students consistently need the following from their college instructors:

- ✓ Consistently communicated expectations of student performance that are reasonable in quantity and quality
- ✓ Sensitivity to the diverse demands on students and reasonable flexibility in accommodating them
- ✓ Effective use of classroom time
- ✓ A classroom environment that includes humor and spontaneity
- ✓ Examinations that address issues properly covered in class and are appropriate to the level of the majority of the students in the class
- ✓ Consistently positive treatment of individual students

The new paradigm of "colleges and universities as service providers to consumer-oriented students" is now firmly entrenched. The successful professor will do well to embrace it.

3   Planning Your Course

(Adapted from Royse, *Teaching Tips for College and University Instructors: A Practical Guide*, published by Allyn & Bacon, Boston, MA, ©2001, by Pearson Education)

Constructing the syllabus: The syllabus should clearly communicate course objectives, assignments, required readings, and grading policies. Think of the syllabus as a stand-alone document. Those students who miss the first or second meeting of a class should be able to learn most of what they need to know about the requirements of the course from reading the syllabus. Start by collecting syllabi from colleagues who have recently taught the course you will be teaching and look for common threads and themes.

Problems to avoid: One mistake commonly made by educators teaching a course for the first time is that they may have rich and intricate visions of how they want students to demonstrate comprehension and synthesis of the material, but they somehow fail to convey this information to those enrolled. Check your syllabus to make sure your expectations have been fully articulated. Be very specific. Avoid vaguely worded instructions:

Instruction	Students may interpret as:
"Write a short paper."	Write a paragraph.
	Write half a page.
	Type a two-page paper.
"Keep a log of your experiences."	Make daily entries.
	Make an entry when the spirit moves me.
	At the end of term, record what I recall.
"Obtain an article from the library."	Any magazine article.
	An article from a professional journal.
	A column from a newsletter.

 Tips for Thriving: Visual Quality

Students today are highly visual learners, so you should give special emphasis to the visual quality of the materials you provide to students. Incorporate graphics into your syllabus and other handouts. Color-code your materials so material for different sections of the course are on different colored papers. Such visuals are likely to create a perception among students that you are contemporary.

4

Your First Class

(Adapted from: Lyons et al, *The Adjunct Professor's Guide to Success*, published by Allyn & Bacon, Boston, MA, ©1999, by Pearson Education)

Success in achieving a great start is almost always directly attributable to the quality and quantity of planning that has been invested by the course professor. If the first meeting of your class is to be successful, you should strive to achieve seven distinct goals.

Create a Positive First Impression: Renowned communications consultant Roger Ailes (1996) claims you have fewer than 10 seconds to create a positive image of yourself. Students are greatly influenced by the visual component; therefore you must look the part of the professional professor. Dress as you would for a professional job interview. Greet each student entering the room. Be approachable and genuine.

Introduce Yourself Effectively: Communicate to students who you are and why you are credible as the teacher of the course. Seek to establish your approachability by "building common ground," such as stating your understanding of students' hectic lifestyles or their common preconceptions toward the subject matter.

Clarify the Goals and Expectations: Make an acetate transparency of each page of the syllabus for display on an overhead projector and using a cover sheet, expose each section as you explain it. Provide clarification and elicit questions.

Conduct an Activity that Introduces Students to Each Other: Students' chances of being able to complete a course effectively is enhanced if each comes to perceive the classmates as a "support network." The small amount of time you invest in an icebreaker will help create a positive classroom atmosphere and pay additional dividends throughout the term.

 Tips for Thriving: Icebreaker

The following activity allows students to get acquainted, exchange opinions, and consider new ideas, values or solutions to problems. It's a great way to promote self-disclosure or an active exchange of viewpoints.

Procedure

1. Give students one or more Post-it™ notes
2. Ask them to write on their note(s) one of the following:
    a. A *value* they hold
    b. An *experience* they have had recently
    c. A *creative idea* or solution to a problem you have posed
    d. A *question* they have about the subject matter of the class
    e. An *opinion* they hold about a topic of your choosing
    f. A *fact* about themselves or the subject matter of the class
3. Ask students to stick the note(s) on their clothing and circulate around the room reading each other's notes.
4. Next, have students mingle once again and negotiate a trade of Post-it™ notes with one another. The trade should be based on a desire to possess a particular value, experience, idea, question, opinion or fact for a short period of time. Set the rule that all trades have to be two-way. Encourage students to make as many trades as they like.
5. Reconvene the class and ask students to share what trades they made and why. (e.g., "I traded for a note that Sally had stating that she has traveled to Eastern Europe. I would really like to travel there because I have ancestors from Hungary and the Ukraine.")

(Adapted from: Silverman, *Active Learning: 101 Strategies to Teach Any Subject*, published by Allyn & Bacon, Boston, MA, ©1996, by Pearson Education).

Learn Students' Names: A student who is regularly addressed by name feels more valued, is invested more effectively in classroom discussion, and will approach the professor with questions and concerns.

Whet Students' Appetite for the Course Material: The textbook adopted for the course is critical to your success. Your first meeting should include a review of its approach, features, and sequencing. Explain to students what percentage of class tests will be derived from material from the textbook.

Reassure Students of the Value of the Course: At the close of your first meeting reassure students that the course will be a valuable learning experience and a wise investment of their time. Review the reasons why the course is a good investment: important and relevant content, interesting classmates, and a dynamic classroom environment.

5   Strategies for Teaching and Learning

(Adapted from: Silverman, *Active Learning: 101 Strategies to Teach Any Subject,* published by Allyn & Bacon, Boston, MA, ©1996, by Pearson Education)

Getting participation through active learning: To learn something well, it helps to hear it, see it, ask questions about it, and discuss it with others. What makes learning "active"? When learning is active, students do most of the work: they use their brains to study ideas, solve problems, and apply what they learn. Active learning is fast-paced, fun, supportive, and personally engaging. Active learning cannot occur without student participation, so there are various ways to structure discussion and obtain responses from students at any time during a class. Here are ten methods to get participation at any time:

1. **Open discussion**. Ask a question and open it up to the entire class without further structuring.
2. **Response cards**. Pass out index cards and request anonymous answers to your questions.
3. **Polling**. Design a short survey that is filled out and tallied on the spot.
4. **Subgroup discussion**. Break students into subgroups of three or more to share and record information.
5. **Learning partners**. Have students work on tasks with the student sitting next to them.
6. **Whips**. Go around the group and obtain short responses to key questions – invite students to pass if they wish.
7. **Panels**. Invite a small number of students to present their views in front of the class.
8. **Fishbowl**. Ask a portion of the class to form a discussion circle and have the remaining students form a listening circle around them. Bring new groups into the inner circle to continue the discussion.
9. **Games**. Use a fun exercise or quiz game to elicit students' ideas, knowledge, or skill.
10. **Calling on the next speaker**. Ask students to raise their hands when they want to share their views and ask the current speaker to choose the next speaker.

(Adapted from Royse, *Teaching Tips for College and University Instructors: A Practical Guide,* published by Allyn & Bacon, Boston, MA, ©2001, by Pearson Education)

Team learning: The essential features of this small group learning approach, developed originally for use in large college classrooms are (1) relatively permanent heterogeneous task groups; (2) grading based on a combination of individual performance, group performance, and peer evaluation; (3) organization of the course so that the majority of class time is spent on small group activities; (4) a six-step instructional process similar to the following model:

1. Individual study of material outside of the class is assigned.
2. Individual testing is used (multiple choice questions over homework at the beginning of class)
3. Groups discuss their answers and then are given a group test of the same items. They then get immediate feedback (answers).
4. Groups may prepare written appeals of items.

5. Feedback is given from instructor.
6. An application-oriented activity is assigned (e.g. a problem to be solved requiring input from all group members).

If you plan to use team learning in your class, inform students at the beginning of the course of your intentions to do so and explain the benefits of small group learning. Foster group cohesion by sitting groups together and letting them choose "identities" such as a team name or slogan. You will need to structure and supervise the groups and ensure that the projects build on newly acquired learning. Make the projects realistic and interesting and ensure that they are adequately structured so that each member's contribution is 25 percent. Students should be given criteria by which they can assess and evaluate the contributions of their peers on a project-by-project basis (Michaelsen, 1994).

 Tips for Thriving: Active Learning and Lecturing

Lecturing is one of the most time-honored teaching methods, but does it have a place in an active learning environment? There are times when lecturing can be effective. Think about the following when planning a lecture:

Build Interest: Capture your students' attention by leading off with an anecdote or cartoon.
Maximize Understanding and Retention: Use brief handouts and demonstrations as a visual backup to enable your students to see as well as hear.
Involve Students during the Lecture: Interrupt the lecture occasionally to challenge students to answer spot quiz questions.
Reinforce the Lecture: Give students a self-scoring review test at the end of the lecture.

---

6   Grading and Assessment Techniques

(Adapted from Wankat, *The Effective, Efficient Professor: Teaching, Scholarship and Service*, published by Allyn & Bacon, Boston, MA, ©2002, by Pearson Education)

Philosophy of grading: Develop your own philosophy of grading by picturing in your mind the performance of typical A students, B students and so on. Try different grading methods until you find one that fits your philosophy and is reasonably fair. Always look closely at students on grade borders – take into account personal factors if the group is small. Be consistent with or slightly more generous than the procedure outlined in your syllabus.

Criterion grading: Professor Philip Wankat writes: "I currently use a form of criterion grading for my sophomore and junior courses. I list the scores in the syllabus that will guarantee the students As, Bs and so forth. For example, a score of 85 to 100 guarantees an A; 75 to 85, a B; 65 to 75, a C; and 55 to 65, a D. If half the class gets above 85% they all get an A. This reduces competition and allows students to work together and help each other. The standard grade gives students something to aim for and tells them exactly what their grade is at any time. For students whose net scores are close to the borders at the end of the course, I look at other factors before deciding a final grade such as attendance."

 Tips for Thriving: Result Feedback

As stated earlier, feedback on results is the most effective of motivating factors. Anxious students are especially hungry for positive feedback. You can quickly and easily provide it by simply writing "Great job!" on the answer sheets or tests. For students who didn't perform well, a brief note such as "I'd love to talk with you at the end of class" can be especially reassuring. The key is to be proactive and maintain high standards, while requiring students to retain ownership of their success.

7 Using Technology

(Adapted from: Sanders, *Creating Learning-Centered Courses for the World Wide Web*, published by Allyn & Bacon, Boston, MA, ©2001, by Pearson Education)

The Web as a source of teaching and learning has generated a great deal of excitement and hyperbole. The Web is neither a panacea nor a demon, but it can be a valuable tool. Among the many misunderstandings about the use of Web pages for teaching and learning is a view that such efforts must encompass an entire course. Like any other tool in a course (e.g. lectures, discussions, films, or field trips) online material can be incorporated to enhance the learning experience.

The best way to start using the Web in a course is with small steps. Developing a single lesson or assignment, a syllabus, or a few well-chosen links makes more sense than trying to develop a whole course without sufficient support or experience. Testing Web materials with a class that regularly meets face-to-face helps a faculty member gauge how well a lesson using the Web works. Making adjustments within the context of a traditional class helps fine-tune Web lessons that may be offered in distance education without face-to-face interaction.

 Tips for Thriving: Using Videos

Generally a videotape should not exceed half and hour in length. Always preview a video before showing it to ensure the content, language, and complexity are appropriate for your students. Include major videos on your syllabus to encourage attendance and integrate them into the context of the course. Plan to evaluate students' retention of the concepts on exams or through reports. Avoid reinforcing the common student perception that watching a video is a time-filler.

By beginning with good practices in learning, we ask not how the new technology can help us do a better job of getting students to learn, but rather we ask how good pedagogy be better implemented with the new technology.

8 Managing Problem Situations

(Adapted from Wankat, *The Effective, Efficient Professor: Teaching, Scholarship and Service*, published by Allyn & Bacon, Boston, MA, ©2002, by Pearson Education)

Cheating: Cheating is one behavior that should not be tolerated. Tolerating cheating tends to make it worse. Prevention of cheating is much more effective than trying to cure it once it has occurred. A professor can prevent cheating by:

- Creating rapport with students
- Gaining a reputation for giving fair tests
- Giving clear instructions and guidelines before, during, and after tests
- Educating students on the ethics of plagiarism
- Requiring periodic progress reports and outlines before a paper is due

Try to develop exams that are perceived as fair and secure by students. Often, the accusation that certain questions were tricky is valid as it relates to ambiguous language and trivial material. Ask your mentor or an experienced instructor to closely review the final draft of your first few exams for these factors.

Tips for Thriving: Discipline

One effective method for dealing with some discipline problems is to ask the class for feedback (Angelo & Cross, 1993) In a one-minute quiz, ask the students, "What can I do to help you learn?" Collate the responses and present them to the class. If behavior such as excessive talking appears in some responses (e.g. "Tell people to shut up") this gives you the backing to ask students to be quiet. Use of properly channeled peer pressure is often effective in controlling undesired behavior

(Adapted from Royse, *Teaching Tips for College and University Instructors: A Practical Guide*, published by Allyn & Bacon, Boston, MA, ©2001, by Pearson Education)

Unmotivated Students: There are numerous reasons why students may not be motivated. The "required course" scenario is a likely explanation – although politics in colonial America is your life's work, it is safe to assume that not everyone will share your enthusiasm. There are also personal reasons such as a death of a loved one or depression. Whenever you detect a pattern that you assume to be due to lack of motivation (e.g. missing classes, not handing assignments in on time, non-participation in class), arrange a time to have the student meet with you outside the classroom. Candidly express your concerns and then listen.

Motivating students is part of the faculty members' job. To increase motivation professors should: show enthusiasm for the topic; use various media and methods to present material; use humor in the classroom; employ activities that encourage active learning; and give frequent, positive feedback.

(Adapted from Baiocco/Waters, *Successful College Teaching*, published by Allyn & Bacon, Boston, MA, ©1998, by Pearson Education)

Credibility Problems. If you are an inexperienced instructor you may have problems with students not taking you seriously. At the first class meeting articulate clear rules of classroom decorum and comport yourself with dignity and respect for students. Try to exude that you are in charge and are the "authority" and avoid trying to pose as the students' friend.

9   Surviving When You're Not Prepared

(Adapted from: Lyons et al, *The Adjunct Professor's Guide to Success*, published by Allyn & Bacon, Boston, MA, ©1999, by Pearson Education)

Despite your thorough course planning, your concern for students, and commitment to the institution, situations will arise – illness, family emergencies – that prevent you from being fully prepared for every class meeting. Most students will excuse one flawed performance during a term, but try to develop contingency plans you can employ on short notice. These might include:

- Recruiting a guest speaker from your circle of colleagues to deliver a presentation that might interest your students.
- Conducting a carousel brainstorming activity, in which a course issue is examined from several perspectives. Divide the students in to groups to identify facts appropriate to each perspective. For example, you might want to do a SWOT analysis (Strengths, Weaknesses, Opportunities, Threats) on a particular organization or public figure.
- Dividing the class into groups of three or four and asking them to develop several questions that would be appropriate for inclusion on your next exam.
- Identify a video at your local rental store that embellishes material from the course.
- Assign students roles (e.g. press, governmental figures, etc.), and conduct a focused analysis of a late-breaking news story related to your course.
- Divide students into groups to work on an assigned course project or upcoming exam.
- As a last resort, admit your inability to prepare a class and allow students input into formulating a strategy for best utilizing class time.

In each case, the key is to shift the initial attention away from yourself (to permit you to gather your thoughts) and onto an activity that engages students in a new and significant way.

10   Improving Your Performance

(Adapted from: Lyons et al, *The Adjunct Professor's Guide to Success*, published by Allyn & Bacon, Boston, MA, ©1999, by Pearson Education)

The instructor who regularly engages in systematic self-evaluation will unquestionably derive greater reward from the formal methods of evaluation commonly employed by colleges and universities. One method for providing structure to an ongoing system of self-evaluation is to keep a journal of reflections on your teaching experiences. Regularly invest 15 or 20 introspective minutes following each class meeting to focus especially on the strategies and events in class that you feel could be improved. Committing your thoughts and emotions enables you to develop more effective habits, build confidence in your teaching performance, and make more effective comparisons later. The following questions will help guide self-assessment:

> *How do I typically begin the class?*
> *Where/How do I position myself in the class?*
> *How do I move in the classroom?*
> *Where are my eyes usually focused?*
> *Do I facilitate students' visual processing of course material?*
> *Do I change the speed, volume, energy, and tone of my voice?*
> *How do I ask questions of students?*
> *How often, and when, do I smile or laugh in class?*
> *How do I react when students are inattentive?*
> *How do I react when students disagree or challenge what I say?*
> *How do I typically end a class?*

 Tips for Thriving: Video-Recording Your Class

In recent years a wide range if professionals have markedly improved their job performance by employing video recorders in their preparation efforts. As an instructor, an effective method might be to ask your mentor or another colleague to tape a 10 to 15 minute mini-lesson then to debrief it using the assessment questions above. Critiquing a videotaped session provides objectivity and is therefore more likely to effect change. Involving a colleague as an informal coach will enable you to gain from their experience and perspective and will reduce the chances of your engaging in self-depreciation.

References

Ailes, R. (1996) *You are the message: Getting what you want by being who you are.* New York: Doubleday.

Chickering, A.W., & Gamson, Z.F. (1987) Seven principles for good practice in undergraduate education. AAHE Bulletin, 39, 3-7.

Michaelson, L.K. (1994). Team Learning: Making a case for the small-group option. In K.W. Prichard & R.M. Sawyer (Eds.), *Handbook of college teaching.* Westport, CT: Greenwood Press.

Sorcinelli, M.D. (1991). Research findings on the seven principles. In A.W. Chickering & Z. Gamson (eds.), *Applying the seven principles of good practice in undergraduate education.* New Directions for Teaching and Learning #47. San Francisco: Jossey-Bass.